# TANZANIA
## in Pictures

Bev Pritchett

Twenty-First Century Books

# Contents

Website address: www.lernerbooks.com

Twenty-First Century Books
A division of Lerner Publishing Group, Inc.
241 First Avenue North
Minneapolis, MN 55401 U.S.A.

web enhanced @ www.vgsbooks.com

## CULTURAL LIFE 46

► Religion. Music and Dance. Visual Arts. Literature.
Media. Sports and Recreation. Holidays. Food.

## THE ECONOMY 56

► Agriculture, Fishing, and Forestry. Main Export
Crops. Zanzibar's Economy. Services,
Transportation, and Communication. Industry
and Imports. Mining and Energy. The Future.

## FOR MORE INFORMATION

Library of Congress Cataloging-in-Publication Data

Pritchett, Bev, 1961–
    Tanzania in pictures / by Bev Pritchett.
        p.   cm. — (Visual geography series)
    Includes bibliographical references and index.
    ISBN 978-0-8225-8571-8 (lib. bdg. : alk. paper)  797/401
        1. Tanzania—Juvenile literature. 2. Tanzania—Pictorial works—Juvenile literature. I. Title.
DT438.P75  2008
967.8—dc22                                              2007022064

Manufactured in the United States of America
1 2 3 4 5 6 – PA – 13 12 11 10 09 08

# INTRODUCTION

The United Republic of Tanzania is a large country in East Africa. The nation consists of a union between two formerly separate countries. The mainland, called Tanganyika, lies on the Indian Ocean coast. A group of offshore islands is collectively known as Zanzibar. The two countries united in 1964. The republic then combined both names to form its new name.

Modern Tanzania is one of the poorest countries in the world. Most of Tanzania's 39 million people live in poverty. About 80 percent of its workers are farmers. Most of them rely on outdated agricultural methods. But the nation is a success in many other ways. While several of its neighbors have suffered civil wars and other violent conflicts, Tanzania's more than 120 ethnic groups live together in peace. Zanzibar experiences some tensions among its Arab, African, Persian, and Asian populations, but generally the union has been a success.

The country's attractions include Africa's highest peak, Mount Kilimanjaro. Reserves such as the Serengeti National Park protect

some of Africa's most spectacular wildlife, including lions, giraffes, and zebras. Every year herds of wildebeest and other antelope trek for miles to find fresh food and water sites. The Olduvai Gorge is the site of fossils and Stone Age tools that suggest the earliest human ancestors lived in Tanzania. These and other sights attract visitors from around the world. Tourism is an important money earner for Tanzania.

Travelers and traders have explored Tanzania's mainland and islands for more than two thousand years. Much of the land's rich and varied history is preserved in its oral tradition (songs and stories), as well as in written form.

For many centuries, foreign powers dominated both regions. By the ninth century, Arab traders had developed Zanzibar into a major Indian Ocean port. The natural resources for their trade, including ivory, gold, and human beings sold as slaves, often came from the mainland. Zanzibar also became a center for growing cloves and other spices in high demand around the world.

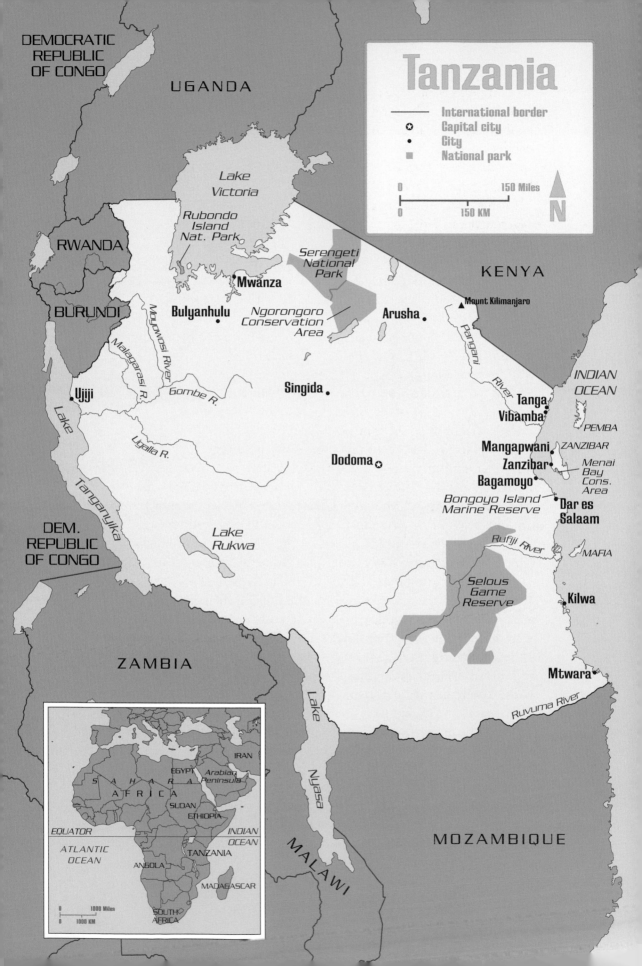

Europeans first began to explore the East African coast in the fifteenth century. The forerunners of modern Tanzanians encountered people from Portugal, Germany, and Great Britain. British colonial agents gained control of both regions by the twentieth century. They introduced the English language and imposed their traditions on the native people. By the 1950s, Africans of both regions were working to gain national independence. The idealistic schoolteacher Julius Nyerere became the hero of the struggle for self-rule.

After winning nationhood, Tanganyika and Zanzibar united to face the problems of economic survival and political instability. The nation's founder, Nyerere, became its first president. Tanzania welcomed economic assistance from China, the United States, Great Britain, and other countries.

Tanzania clearly established its strong African identity when the nation chose Swahili (also known as Kiswahili) instead of English as its official language. Nyerere's economic programs, however, had driven the nation to bankruptcy by the time he retired in 1985. The reform of his successors allowed Tanzania to gradually advance.

The deadly human immunodeficiency virus (HIV), the virus that often causes acquired immunodeficiency syndrome (AIDS), first hit Tanzania hard in the 1980s and slowed the nation's progress. Limited health-care and educational systems challenged the country. The poor nation also struggled to improve inadequate roads, sanitation systems, and other public works. Tanzania is generally a peaceful country, but many of its neighbors have suffered civil wars and other violent conflicts. These conflicts have sometimes affected Tanzania negatively.

Tanzania continues to face these and other challenges in the twenty-first century. The nation's citizens elected President Jakaya Kikwete in 2005, in a democratic multiparty race. He and his government are committed to improving Tanzania's economy and social services. The country's motto is *Uhuru na Umoja*, which means "Freedom and Unity" in Swahili. Despite the instability of the region, Tanzanians together pursue these values.

# THE LAND

The United Republic of Tanzania covers 364,881 square miles (945,037 sq. kilometers). It is about the size of Texas and Oklahoma combined. The area includes the mainland and the 640 square miles (1,658 sq. km) of Zanzibar, Pemba, Mafia, and other smaller, scattered islands in the Indian Ocean. These islands are known all together as Zanzibar.

Located in East Africa, the nation is just below the equator (the midway point between the North Pole and the South Pole). Tanzania shares borders with Uganda and Kenya to the north. The mainland's eastern boundary is the Indian Ocean. Zambia, Malawi, and Mozambique lie to the south. Rwanda, Burundi, and the Democratic Republic of Congo (formerly Zaire) border Tanzania to the west.

## ◉ The Mainland

The mainland, known as Tanganyika, rises from the Indian Ocean. Its topography, or landscape, is greatly varied. It consists of coastal plains, a central plateau (elevated plain), and highlands in the north and south.

The Great Rift Valley is a series of cracks, or rifts, in the earth. The valley helped form large lakes, volcanic areas, and mountains in Tanzania. It runs for thousands of miles from southwestern Asia down the eastern length of Africa, including Tanzania. The Great Rift Valley branches off into the Western Rift Valley in Tanzania.

The Coastal Plain region extends inland from the Indian Ocean for up to 40 miles (64 km). Tanzania's former capital and largest city, Dar es Salaam, sits on the hot and humid coast. The 500-mile- (800-km) long coastline can be dangerous for ships because of its many coral reefs and sandbars. (Coral reefs are made of the skeletons of tiny sea animals.)

The Central Plateau region gradually rises about 3,500 feet (1,067 meters) above the coast. This large, high plain lies between the Great Rift Valley and the Western Rift Valley. Its hot and dry climate supports only low-level vegetation.

The Serengeti Plain is a vast savanna (grassland) in the north. The plain holds the Serengeti National Park, one of the world's most

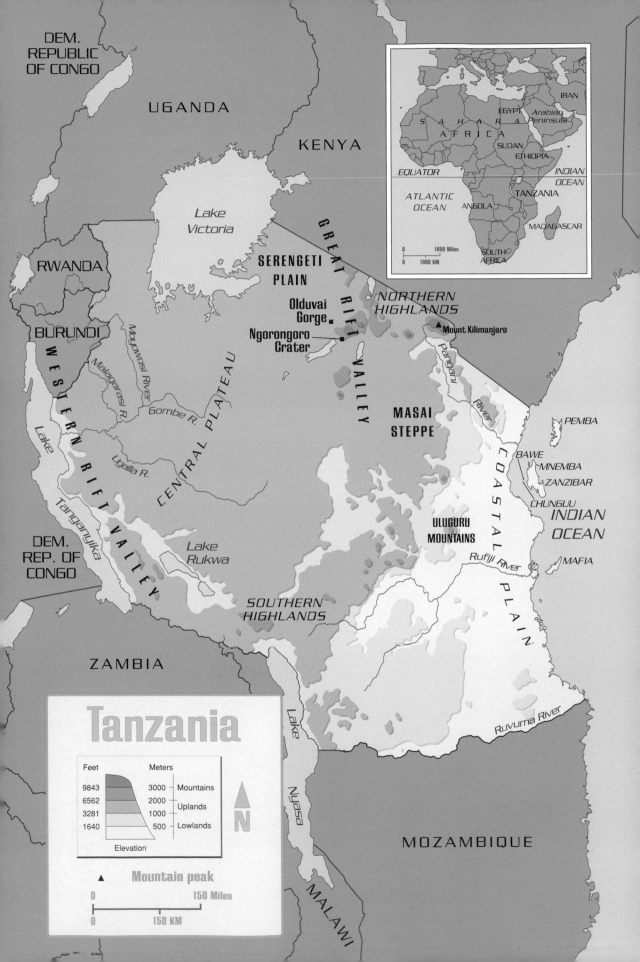

famous wildlife preserves. Tourists on safari see familiar African animals such as lions and zebras there. The Masai Steppe in the north is another dominant feature. The Masai (also spelled Maasai) people have grazed their cattle on the grasslands for many generations.

The mountains of the Northern Highlands region include Mount Kilimanjaro. It is the African continent's highest point, at 19,340 feet (5,895 m). As the altitude increases, the weather cools. Snow and icy glaciers cap Kilimanjaro all year.

## NO SNOWS ON KILIMANJARO?

*Kilimanjaro* means "mountain of snow," and its snowcapped peak is an awesome sight. Traditional local beliefs name the mountain as the place where God lives. The snow and ice provide water for the local Chaga people. But the ice cover is melting. Studies show that more than 80 percent of the ice has melted since 1912. At the current rate of decline, the ice fields may be gone completely by 2025. The reasons behind the dwindling ice fields are complex, but human factors are partly to blame. These include deforestation (loss of woodlands) and global warming (rising temperatures on Earth, due partly to pollution). The mountain attracts more tourists than any other place in Tanzania. Once the snows are gone, economists worry that the twenty thousand tourists who come to climb or view the awesome mountain every year will be gone too.

Mount Kilimanjaro towers over a pair of acacia trees in Tanzania.

Ngorongoro Conservation Area also lies in the Northern Highlands. This park encompasses an extinct volcano. The volcano is 12 miles (19 km) in diameter. Its collapsed walls are about 7,000 feet (2,100 m) high. Its floor lies 2,000 feet (600 m) below the level of the surrounding ground. Wildlife abounds in the crater. The conservation area also contains the Olduvai Gorge. This gorge, or canyon, runs for about 30 miles (48 km) at a depth of about 328 feet (98 m). It is the site of many ancient fossils, including bones of the earliest known human ancestors.

The Uluguru Mountains mark the beginning of the Southern Highlands region. The highlands run westward from Lake Nyasa (also called Lake Malawi) eastward to Tanzania's coast. Near Lake Nyasa, mountains and grasslands characterize the landscape. The Selous Game Reserve east of the lake is the largest game reserve in Africa. The region's coastal side consists of hills and rock outcroppings.

## The Islands

The archipelago (group of islands) known as Zanzibar takes its name from the largest island. Zanzibar Island (also called Ungaja) lies 22 miles (35 km) off Tanzania's mainland. It is 50 miles (80 km) long and 25 miles (40 km) at its widest point. Traders have operated out of its ports for centuries. The western part of Zanzibar is hilly and slowly descends into a plain.

The other islands lie a few miles farther off the mainland coast. Pemba is a steep, hilly island just a few miles north of Zanzibar. Mafia is a low island about 100 miles (161 km) to the south. Smaller islands include Bawe, Chunguu, and Mnemba.

The archipelago is a popular vacation spot, with white sand beaches and warm Indian Ocean waters. Acres of spice plants scent the air with cloves, nutmeg, and vanilla.

## Lakes and Rivers

Three extraordinary inland bodies of water—three of Africa's Great Lakes—border Tanzania. Two of these are very deep, relatively narrow lakes formed within the Western Rift Valley. Lake Nyasa lies within Malawi but forms part of Tanzania's southwestern border. Lake Tanganyika marks the country's western border and lies partly in Tanzania.

By volume, Lake Tanganyika is the third-largest freshwater lake in the world. The lake's floor is the deepest point on the African continent. Its overall depth is 4,730 feet (1,442 m). But because the Great Rift's walls hold the waters high above sea level, the lake only reaches 2,300 feet (690 m) below sea level.

A landmark in Mwanza, Tanzania, is Bismarck's Rock in **Lake Victoria.**

In the north is the third Great Lake. Lake Victoria spreads over the boundaries of Tanzania, Uganda, and Kenya. Covering 26,828 square miles (69,484 sq. km), Lake Victoria is the second-largest freshwater lake by area in the world. (Lake Superior in North America is the first.) Lake Victoria is 3,700 feet (1,128 m) above sea level because the branches of the Great and Western rifts hold it high. It reaches only 270 feet (81 m) in depth. Lake Victoria is a main source of the Nile River, the longest river in the world. The Nile flows northward from the lake. It travels through Uganda, Sudan, and Egypt before emptying into the Mediterranean Sea. Though not a Great Lake, Lake Rukwa is a large lake in southwestern Tanzania.

Lake Tanganyika receives several western Tanzanian rivers—such as the Malagarasi and its tributary (branch), the Moyowosi. The rivers' waters eventually find their way to the Atlantic Ocean on the western side of the continent. Rivers that flow eastward to the Indian Ocean include the Rufiji, the Pangani, and the Ruvuma. They provide water for irrigation (artificial watering systems) for farmers. Dams on the rivers harness the power of rushing water to produce hydroelectricity.

## Climate

Because Tanzania is in the Southern Hemisphere (south of the equator), seasons there are the reverse of seasons in the Northern Hemisphere. But because Tanzania is so close to the equator, the temperature does not vary much between seasons. Dar es Salaam, on the coast, averages 82°F (28°C) in the summer month of January. The winter month of July is only a few degrees cooler, with an average temperature of 74°F (23°C). On the coast and the islands, temperatures sometimes exceed 90°F (32°C). Sea breezes temper the heat and high humidity (level of moisture in the air).

Equatorial regions are the world's hottest, but inland Tanzania's high altitude cools the air. Dodoma on the Central Plateau averages 75°F (24°C) in January and 67°F (19°C) in July. The temperate highlands average 68°F (20°C). Most of the year, temperatures are freezing cold on the top of Mount Kilimanjaro.

Tanzania experiences one or two rainy seasons. Seasonal winds blow heavy rains from the northeast between October and February. December is the rainiest month in most of the country. Winds blow from the southwest during the rest of the year. In the highlands and along the coast, a second rainy season begins in March or April. Rainfall in Tanzania averages 44 inches (112 centimeters) per year along the coast and around Lake Victoria. It dwindles to 10 inches (25 cm) per year in the Central Plateau. Flooding during the rainy season is a concern on the Central Plateau, where heavy rains regularly wash away fertile soil. The rest of the year, drought, or times of little or no rainfall, can be a problem.

## Flora and Fauna

Tanzania's wildly varied plants and animals reflect the country's many landscapes. Zanzibar is well known for its spice plants, especially cloves. This spice comes from the dried flower bud of a tropical tree. On the coasts of the mainland and islands, coconut palms, banana plants, and cashew trees are plentiful. Mangrove trees live in swampy coastal regions. Their partially aboveground roots can tolerate the salty water there.

West of the mainland's coastal strip and extending about 20 miles (32 km) inland lies a wilderness of scrub vegetation, dry riverbeds, rocky hills, and giant baobab trees. People use baobabs' sour fruit, leaves, and bark for food, medicine, and building materials.

Much of the interior consists of sparse, dry woodland called *miombo*. The interior also supports vast grasslands dotted with thorny acacia trees. Lush forests grow in the highlands. On the mountain slopes, thick rain forests start at about 5,000 feet (1,500 m) above sea level. Types of trees include yellowwood and various species of cedar. Near the highest peaks, bamboo and groundsels grow plentifully. Groundsels look like giant cabbages. They can grow to be 18 feet (6 m) high. The plant commonly known as the African violet originally grew only in Tanzania's rain forest.

Tanzania is famous for its wild animals, including giraffes, warthogs, zebras, jackals, leopards, buffalo, and rhinoceroses. Ngorongoro Crater is the home of the largest permanent population of game animals in Africa. The crater's residents include lions, cheetahs, and hyenas. Endangered chimpanzees and gorillas live in western forests. Different kinds of baboons and other monkeys are common in the country. The rare red colobus monkey lives on Zanzibar Island.

**Lions** lounge together in Serengeti National Park.

Hippopotamuses and crocodiles inhabit streams and riverbanks.

Serengeti National Park covers 5,600 square miles (14,500 sq. km) of northern Tanzania. It is almost as large as Connecticut. The land varies between grasslands and thick forest. The park protects a huge wildlife population. The large game animals include one million wildebeests (gnus). The name of these oxlike animals means "wild ox" in Afrikaans (a language of South Africa). They are actually one of Tanzania's thirty kinds of antelope. Large herds of wildebeests, gazelles, and other antelope move each year toward new water and food supplies. The Selous Game Reserve protects fifty thousand elephants and the endangered African hunting dog.

Tanzania hosts more than one thousand kinds of birds. Thousands of flamingos turn the air pink as they rise from the Ngorongoro Crater. Tanzania's birdlife also includes parrots, ostriches, and pelicans. Wading birds such as storks and herons inhabit swampy areas.

Tanzania's lakes hold more than two hundred kinds of water animals, including rare mollusks and crustaceans. The waters off Zanzibar teem with sea life. Kingfish, barracuda, and tuna are among the favorite big catches. Several kinds of dolphins frolic in the warm waters. Endangered sea turtles come onto island beaches to lay their eggs. Low tide on the beach reveals small pools of starfish, minnows, and anemones.

## HONK-BARKING MONKEYS

In 2005 scientists discovered a monkey species in the mountain forests of southern Tanzania. The kipunji, also known as the highland mangabey, lives in trees at altitudes as high as 8,000 feet (2,450 m) above sea level. Its long, brown fur protects it from cold. Researchers describe the kipunji's soft call as a "honk-bark." The kipunji is more closely related to members of the baboon family than to other kinds of mangabeys, which communicate in loud "whoop-gobbles." Illegal logging has destroyed some of the monkey's habitat, and no more than one thousand kipunjis remain.

A fishing crew landed a **coelacanth** near Zanzibar on July 14, 2007. The rare coelacanth is nicknamed the fossil fish because it belongs to a class of fish that appeared about 350 to 400 million years ago, predating dinosaurs. Go to www.vgsbooks.com for links to information about the history of the coelacanth in Africa.

## Natural Resources

Tanzania enjoys an ample supply of water, with three large lakes, the Indian Ocean coastline, rivers, and wetlands. This resource offers fishing, hydroelectric power, transportation routes, and water for people, farming, and industry. Tanzania's mineral resources include gold, diamonds and other gemstones, coal, natural gas, iron ore, phosphates (used in fertilizer), soda ash, and salt. The country's wildlife, beautiful scenery, and interesting historical sights attract tourists. Visitors bring much-needed money into the struggling economy.

## Environmental Issues

Poverty is the root of many of Tanzania's environmental concerns. Poor people poach (illegally hunt) animals to feed their families. Other poachers kill elephants, zebras, and other animals to sell their valuable ivory tusks or skins. Often lacking electricity, rural Tanzanians cut down trees and brush for cooking and heating fuel. Loggers also strip vegetation. Deforestation leads to a spiral of environmental destruction. As trees are cut down, there are fewer roots to hold the soil in place. Wind blows and rain washes dirt away. This process is called soil erosion. It leads to desertification, or the process of land turning to drylands. Drought speeds up the spread of desert lands.

The practice of fishing with dynamite (killing fish with explosives) destroys coral reefs. This destruction is another of the nation's main environmental concerns. The loss of coral reefs threatens the marine life that lives there. The government has established some marine parks to protect the fragile coasts. Water pollution from sewage, fertilizer runoff, and industry further damages the ocean environment.

Overlarge populations of big game animals, floods, and severe dry seasons also challenge the balance of nature in Tanzania. The Tanzanian government works to balance the population's need for farmland with the animals' need for space. The government runs twelve national parks and thirteen game preserves, where many animals live in their natural surroundings. Nongovernmental organizations also work to protect the environment. The Tanzania Forest Conservation Group, for instance, helps villagers raise and plant young trees to help stop deforestation. However, 143 kinds of animals and 236 kinds of plants are endangered or threatened with dying out completely.

An adult shows a group of Tanzanian youth how to plant trees. **Reforestation** is important for protecting Tanzania's wildlife populations.

# ▶ Cities

Tanzania is largely a farming nation. Only 32 percent of its citizens live in towns and cities. Many of its most important cities were originally trading stations along ancient trade routes.

DAR ES SALAAM (population 2.5 million) is Tanzania's former capital. It lies on the coast of Tanzania's mainland, just south of Zanzibar Island. The sultan (ruler) of Zanzibar founded the city in the 1860s. Its Arabic name means "haven of peace." The sultan wanted to create a refuge for himself, away from Zanzibar.

Dar es Salaam is the crowded hub for much of the country's activity. Though Dodoma has been the capital since 1974, many government workers and offices remain in Dar es Salaam. The city is also Tanzania's commercial, transportation, and financial center. It is home to Africans, Arabs, East Indians, and Europeans.

MWANZA (population 400,000) is an important port city on Lake Victoria's southern shore. Products from the area's tea, cotton, citrus fruit, and coffee plantations (large farms) pass though Mwanza on their way to market. Boats cross Lake Victoria to Kenya and Uganda.

**Dar es Salaam,** once the capital city of Tanzania, remains the country's business hub.

Visitors to the western Serengeti stop in Mwanza. The Sukuma, the largest ethnic group in Tanzania, have farmed the region near Mwanza for centuries. Gold mines are the region's biggest money earner.

ARUSHA (population 271,000) in the northern highlands is a tourism center for visitors going to nearby Serengeti National Park, Mount Kilimanjaro, and Ngorongoro Crater. Germans established the city as a center of their colonial rule in the early 1900s. The area's fertile soil supports coffee, corn, and cattle raising. Arusha has become a center of Tanzanian international relations and diplomacy. For instance, the United Nations chose Arusha as the site of its court of justice for trials on the 1994 genocide, or ethnic mass murders, in Rwanda. It is also the western end point for the Tanga railway.

ZANZIBAR CITY (population 250,000) is located on Zanzibar Island. The deepwater port city displays a mixture of cultures. In what is called Stone Town, the architecture and narrow streets reflect Arab influence. This section of the city contrasts sharply with Ngambo, which means "the other side," largely an African settlement of mud dwellings. Cloves remain an important export, but tourism is Zanzibar's leading earner.

TANGA (population 220,000) is Tanzania's northeastern deepwater port. Arab traders founded the city in the fourteenth century. The Tanga railway line extends into the country's northern agricultural region. The railway also provides access to the national parks of north central Tanzania. Tanga exports local produce, including cotton and coffee. It also ships goods made in the city, such as steel, plywood, and rope.

DODOMA (population 170,000) is named for the word *idodomya*, which means "sinking place." The name refers to a legend about an elephant sinking in a swamp near the city. Historically, merchants traveling from the coast toward Lake Tanganyika stopped at Dodoma. Rich farm fields and pleasant scenery surround Dodoma. The government chose the centrally located city to become the new capital in 1974. The transfer of Tanzania's legislature, the National Assembly, to Dodoma is complete, but much government remains in Dar es Salaam.

Visit www.vgsbooks.com for links to learn more about the urban, rural, and wild landscapes of Tanzania.

# HISTORY AND GOVERNMENT

The beginning of the known history of Tanzania involves the Olduvai Gorge. Here, British anthropologists Mary and Louis Leakey found bone fragments, including pieces of skull, and tools. These findings suggest that ancestors of the human family lived in the region 2.3 million years ago. As a result of the Olduvai discoveries, many consider Africa (and Tanzania in particular) to be the original home of humankind.

## Early Migrations

People from western Africa had migrated to present-day Tanzania by 10,000 B.C. These immigrants, the Khoikhoi and the San, survived by hunting wild animals and gathering plants. They spoke "click-tongue" languages (employing sounds made by clicking the tongue) still found in southern Africa. About 1000 B.C., different groups entered mainland Tanzania from the north. These peoples from central Sudan and from the region east of the Nile were cattle herders.

Bantu-speaking people began to move into the region from the northwest about two thousand years ago. *Bantu* means "people." These newer immigrants were farmers. Unlike the people already settled in the region, they knew how to forge iron into tools and weapons.

About the same time, Roman traders reached the coast of East Africa. Soon the coast and islands of East Africa were trading ivory and other goods with seafaring merchants from lands as far away as China.

## Arab Traders

Traders from the Arabian Peninsula began arriving on the islands and coasts of present-day Tanzania in the A.D. 700s. Within one hundred years, Arab merchants had come to dominate the large Indian Ocean trading business. They also brought their language, Arabic, and their religion, Islam.

At this time, Nilotic peoples (from the regions around the Nile River) moved south into Tanzania. Among these cattle herders were the ancestors of the modern Luo and Masai peoples.

By the 1100s, traders and settlers had arrived from Persia (modern Iran). The traders were largely from Shiraz. This Persian city controlled the eastern half of the Persian Gulf. Shirazis followed either the Islamic faith or the ancient Persian religion Zoroastrianism. Indian merchants also sailed to the African coast from the trading center of Delhi, India.

Cities and trading posts sprang up all along the East African coast. These settlements were independent and formed no unified empire. Occasionally, more powerful settlements would demand tribute, or payments, from weaker ones. The main trading posts were Kilwa along the southern Tanzanian coast, Bagamoyo farther north, and Zanzibar. Foreign merchants traded cloth, iron implements, glass, and decorative items for African ivory from elephant trunks and human slaves. Foreign traders took the goods and slaves to Arab and East Indian lands. Kilwa also controlled the trade in gold from present-day Mozambique to the south.

**The East African coast was a major site for shipping out enslaved Africans. Tanzania's port city Bagamoyo (modern population 80,000) was one of the region's most important ports. Its name is said to mean "throw down your heart" in Swahili. It refers to the slaves' loss of hope that, from this point on, they would ever see their homes again.**

The earliest missionaries, or religious teachers, to come to East Africa were Arab Muslims (followers of Islam). But few Islamic teachers came with the trading ships. Muslim traders were not active in seeking converts among inland peoples because Islam forbids one Muslim from enslaving another. Arab traders knew that conversion of the local peoples to Islam would prevent traders taking converted Africans as slaves.

Meanwhile, Africans inland largely continued to follow their traditional religions. The religions generally shared a belief that spirit, or conscious life, inhabits natural objects, such as mountains and rivers, and natural events, such as illness and the weather. The spirits of ancestors were also seen to be powerful forces.

For five centuries, the Arab trading system dominated the coast and the islands. An African-Arab culture thrived. It is called Swahili, which means "people of the coast." The Swahili language, a blend of Arab and Bantu languages, developed. Arab culture influenced the cultural, commercial, and social patterns during this period. Many people on the coasts and Zanzibar adopted Islam. The Swahili traders had a less direct impact on interior regions of Tanzania because the terrain there was too difficult for them to settle.

## Portuguese Influences

At the close of the fifteenth century, Arab Muslims were blocking routes Europeans used to reach markets to the east. Looking for alternative trade routes to India, Vasco da Gama sailed from Portugal around the southern tip of Africa. The explorer's voyage began in 1497. By 1498 he had reached the East African coast. He observed the rich trading settlements. His reports caused much excitement at the Portuguese royal court.

Greed for gold, ivory, and slaves, as well as a desire to harm their Muslim enemies, motivated the Christian Portuguese to wage war for control of the East African coast. The Portuguese and the Arabs alternately dominated the trade routes, depending on who was victorious in battle during a given year.

In the 1650s, Arabs from Oman in southern Arabia took control of Zanzibar. It became the center of the slave trade. From Zanzibar, Omani control reached into the coast and interior of the mainland.

By 1698 the Arabs and their allies had been able to drive out the Portuguese with a series of counterattacks. Zanzibar became part of the sultanate (kingdom) of Oman. Once more the Tanzanian coast came under complete Arab domination. Although the conflict between the Arabs and the Portuguese destroyed some trading posts, many of these strongholds were rebuilt and soon thrived again.

> The Arabs who sailed to East Africa called the coast and the offshore islands **Zinj el Barr**, which means "Land of the Blacks" in Arabic. The name was in use when the Portuguese arrived. Afterward, "Zanzibar" began to refer only to the islands.

## Arab Revival

After the Arabs had reestablished control over the coast of East Africa, the Arab pattern of trading and slavery flourished. Newly developed plantations on the islands and elsewhere relied on slaves. The slave markets of the Middle East and Africa were strong, and many Europeans took part in the slave trade. The British people opposed slavery, however, and their government outlawed the trade in slaves in 1807.

Under the Arab sultan of Zanzibar, Seyyid Said (1804–1856), Zanzibar become the gateway to trade with the whole coast of East Africa. The British courted Said. They hoped to persuade the sultan to outlaw the slave trade along the East African coast. The British also wanted to increase trade and to curb French influence in the region. Although the sultan entered into some minor agreements with the

British, the slave trade continued. Great Britain outlawed slave owning throughout its empire in 1833.

In 1840 Sultan Said moved his capital from Muscat, Oman, to the island of Zanzibar. He encouraged settlers from India to move and work there. He also encouraged the use of slave labor to develop plantations for growing cloves. Ships came for cloves and other spices from as far away as the United States.

## European Explorations

During the mid-nineteenth century, European interest in the continent of Africa grew stronger after the publication of reports from a new wave of explorers. East Africa became the destination of frequent European expeditions. The journeys of explorers and Christian missionaries supplied maps and information about East Africa.

In the 1840s, the first groups of European missionaries arrived in East Africa. They sought to convert Africans to the Christian religion. Many also worked to end slavery. Two German missionaries reached Mount Kilimanjaro in the 1840s. But Tanzania's harsh terrain and dangerous diseases, such as malaria, often lessened missionaries' zeal. Those who survived set up missions in densely populated areas. They concentrated their efforts on converting the elders and local leaders, called chiefs. The missionaries thought that if the chiefs became Christian, the rest of the community would follow.

The missionaries introduced European-style education and health practices to the region. The missionary movement also tried to decrease the slave trade and increase legal forms of trade.

**Workers dry cloves on a Zanzibar plantation** in the 1800s.

In 1857 British explorers Richard Burton and John Speke reached the shores of Lake Tanganyika. In the late 1860s, Scottish missionary David Livingstone began to explore the area near the lake. Livingstone's discoveries about African people and places especially spurred European interest in East Africa.

**Richard Burton**

European powers developed ambitions to colonize, or control, the continent. They hoped to gain control of Africa's raw materials for Europe's fast-expanding industries. East Africa became the arena for international colonial competition.

By 1876 the British had convinced the sultan of Zanzibar, the son of Said, to stop trading (but not to stop owning) slaves. They had threatened to blockade the island otherwise. After the slave trade ended, commerce in cloves, ivory, and rubber increased.

## German Rule

Germany developed its colonial empire in East Africa largely through the efforts of Carl Peters. He was the head of the Society for German Colonization. In 1884 Peters made a six-week journey through the interior of the mainland. He signed a dozen treaties with local leaders. Though they were not always legal, these treaties became the basis for German colonial claims as Europe prepared for the quick division of the continent.

At European conferences, Europeans established rules for colonization of Africa. Different leaders staked their claims to different parts of the continent. As a result of an agreement made with Great Britain, France, and Belgium in 1890, Germany gained control of present-day Rwanda, Burundi, and mainland Tanzania. Land to the north of the middle of Lake Victoria went to the British. Land to the south went to Germany. Together, Germany's colonial holdings were called German East Africa.

All of these plans were made without asking African leaders. The partitioning of Africa ignored the region's ethnic groups. The divisions also drew borders in places where none had existed before.

The German government placed a private firm, the German East Africa Company, in charge of its colonies. Its administration proved to be harsh. The company divided East Africa into large German-owned plantations to produce cash crops to sell abroad. It forced Africans to work for the planters. Its land policies conflicted with local, age-old African practices. Traditionally, the related members of a village worked the community's farmland, and they shared the fruits of their labor. But the Europeans took over the land and paid Africans wages. The

**A sultan from Tanganyika** served as an official of the German government while Dar es Salaam was the capital of German East Africa from 1891 to 1916.

Europeans also used forced labor to build roads and railways. Working conditions were harsh, and pay was low.

Concern arose in Germany when Africans began protesting the unfair conditions. Finally, in 1891, the German government took over control of the territory. Germany headquartered the colonial governor in Dar es Salaam.

Although the British had stopped the trading of slaves, slavery still existed in East Africa. Laws abolished slavery on Zanzibar in 1897. But loopholes in the laws made actual freedom for the African slaves unlikely. The Arab need for a cheap labor force meant slavery continued on the islands. The German colonial governor allowed African slaves to buy their freedom after 1901. He also decreed that children of slaves born after 1906 would be free.

German government officials were no more skillful in running the colony than private administrators had been. But they had military power to stop uprisings against colonial rule.

The most famous and largest uprising was the Maji-Maji Revolt (1905–1907). Its name came from a religious ritual meant to protect African warriors. For the first time, different African ethnic groups united to fight for self-rule. For two years, they fought in the south against Germany's forced-work policy and its poor treatment of African workers. The Germans burned hundreds of villages to put

Learn more about Tanzania's history and people by going to www.vgsbooks.com for links.

down the rebellion. By the end, an estimated 120,000 Africans had died of fighting or starvation.

News of the revolt and of the unfair labor conditions that led to it concerned the people of Germany. Therefore, Germany established a new policy protecting African rights. German administrators allowed African workers to continue their traditional way of farming. They no longer forced them to work for Europeans. Nevertheless, plantation owners found enough African workers to continue doing the hard manual labor.

In Zanzibar, slavery finally came to an end in 1911. Without jobs or government assistance, however, the newly freed people on the islands continued to live in poverty.

## British Control

When tensions in Europe erupted into World War I (1914–1918), the war spilled over into European colonies in Africa. Little economic production and even less trade took place during these years. Many Africans died of starvation, and many others died in battle.

Germany surrendered at the end of the war. The winning nations broke up Germany's colonial empire. The League of Nations, a newly formed international peacekeeping organization, oversaw mainland Tanzania. The league placed it under British control. At this time, the mainland region was officially named Tanganyika.

Slavery was completely abolished after the British gained control of Tanganyika. Farming recovered from wartime losses and went beyond prewar levels. Educational opportunities grew under British supervision.

The British employed local African leaders to govern much of the territory for them. But Africans did not want their chiefs to become colonial agents. Many refused to follow chiefs who worked for the British.

Several all-African organizations formed in the 1920s to pursue rights for Africans. The first was the Tanganyikan African Civil Service Union. In 1929 the African Association formed. A branch opened on Zanzibar in 1934. Neither group enjoyed much political influence at the time.

The worldwide Depression (1929–1942) hit East Africa hard. The economy and social services such as schools suffered for lack of money during this decade.

Meanwhile, Zanzibar remained an Arab territory. Arab owners used Africans as the labor force on their clove and coconut plantations on the islands. The Arabs largely kept both the Africans and the Shirazis (people of Persian heritage, usually mixed with African) from gaining political power and schooling. The Shirazis formed an association in 1939 to promote their social and economic welfare. The Arabs and East Indians also formed their own organizations during this time.

# World War II and the Rise of Nationalism

When World War II (1939–1945) erupted in Europe, once again conflict among colonial powers spread to Africa. Eighty thousand Tanganyikans joined the British forces fighting against Germany, Japan, and their allies. The Tanganyikans served in campaigns in North Africa, Madagascar (in the Indian Ocean), and in the British colony of Burma (modern Myanmar) in Southeast Asia. Because the Japanese gained control of the supply of sisal (used to make rope) and rubber from Southeast Asia, Britain and its allies relied partially on East Africa for these items.

The British allowed local African leaders even more authority during the war. Some misused their power and became unpopular with their people.

After Germany's defeat in World War II, Tanganyika became a United Nations (UN) trust territory. As a trust, Tanganyika was still under British rule. But the goal of the UN's trusteeship was to prepare Tanganyika for self-rule. The UN sent fact-finding missions to Tanganyika every three years to make sure local people were more involved in running their country.

African nationalists, or people who support self-rule for a nation, began to develop political power in 1948. That year the African Association (AA) split with its Zanzibari branch and became the Tanganyikan African Association (TAA). The TAA focused on local concerns, such as farming policies.

During its first two decades, the AA had gained little public support

## THE TANGANYIKA GROUNDNUT SCHEME

The Tanganyika Groundnut Scheme was the British government's attempt to grow peanuts—called groundnuts in Africa—in Tanganyika after World War II. The peanuts were to supply vegetable oil to Great Britain, where there was a shortage. The project met with troubles from the start. Workers struggled to move heavy equipment on Tanganyika's dirt roads. They faced floods, drought, and wild animals to clear miles of thorn bushes and dig up heavy clay soil. The tangled mass of roots made root-cutter blades dull within hours. Local killer bees stung workers, who had to be hospitalized. Furthermore, it turned out that the chosen site was not good for growing peanuts. Workers planted 4,000 tons (3,628 metric tons) of seed peanuts. After two years, they harvested 2,000 tons (1,814 metric tons)—only half of the original seed peanuts. The British government gave up the job as a total loss in 1951. The $50 million scheme remains a famous failure in the history of late colonialism.

and had had little effect on political events. In 1953, however, the TAA elected a young schoolteacher named Julius Nyerere as its president. This idealistic man set about reforming the organization. He envisioned a nation of men and women who would set aside African ethnic and class divisions and work together for shared goals.

Under Nyerere's leadership, the TAA wrote a new constitution and changed its name to the Tanganyikan African National Union (TANU). Nyerere hoped to gain recognition for the party among all Africans, not just among a small, educated group. TANU's goals included agricultural reform and free elections.

Meanwhile, concerned that TANU would exclude Europeans from power, the British authorities in Tanganyika started a campaign against TANU and its leaders. British authorities refused to allow public TANU meetings and rallies. Discrimination against active TANU members kept them from getting government jobs. TANU was outlawed in certain districts as a threat to law and order. TANU continued nonetheless. TANU members held secret meetings and distributed literature around the country despite the colonial government's opposition.

In contrast to a relatively peaceful independence movement in Tanganyika, Zanzibar had a stormy road to self-rule. The ethnic, religious, and cultural divisions and distrust among the islands' people led to conflict. One of the major groups in Zanzibar was the Shirazis, whose Persian ancestors began arriving in Zanzibar as far back as the tenth century. Another group consisted of Africans of mainland ancestry. A small East Indian community also lived on the island. They engaged mainly in commerce and finance. The most powerful people in Zanzibar, however, were the Arabs. This minority group had long ruled Zanzibar. Arabs lived mostly in the cities, and many had grown wealthy through trade.

To prevent Arab domination when national independence arrived, Africans and Shirazis joined to form what finally became the Afro-Shirazi Party (ASP). The Arabs organized the Zanzibar Nationalist Party (ZNP). In 1954 the Arabs began to maneuver for independent control of the islands. They began to refuse to cooperate with the British colonial government.

## ◉ Julius Nyerere and TANU

Julius Nyerere and the leaders of TANU presented their case for independence to the UN mission in 1954. The party leadership also pointed out that poverty and lack of schooling hampered Tanganyika's economic and social progress.

The UN mission suggested 1975 as a target date for independence. To maintain the support of the UN mission, Julius Nyerere flew to New York to speak before the UN General Assembly. Nyerere demanded free elections and increased African participation in the government of the trusteeship. He impressed many UN members with his moderate policies. He promised, for example, full citizenship and participation for Asians and Europeans living in Tanganyika after independence.

On October 22, 1959, Julius Nyerere addressed his country's newly elected lawmakers. He said, "We, the people of Tanganyika, would like to light a candle and put it on top of Mount Kilimanjaro which would shine beyond our borders giving hope where there was despair, love where there was hate and dignity where before there was only humiliation." His famous speech became known as "A Candle on Kilimanjaro."

Tanganyika's colonial administration responded by trying to downplay the importance of TANU. But by then, TANU counted 250,000 supporters. Tanganyika held its first general elections in 1958 and 1959. Tanganyikans elected members to the Legislative Council (a lawmaking body with limited power). TANU won a majority in several provinces.

After the elections of 1958–1959, the hope of independence prompted TANU to cooperate with colonial authorities. The new colonial governor of Tanganyika was Richard Turnbull. He desired a peaceful transition to independence. Governor Turnbull created great excitement when he announced in December 1959 that Tanganyika would have some sort of self-government within the following year.

The last UN mission came to Tanganyika in 1960. The mission reported that the country would achieve its independence as early as possible despite the serious economic problems that Tanganyika faced.

After TANU won a majority in another election in 1960, Governor Turnbull asked Julius Nyerere to form a government. A constitutional conference met in London in March 1961. The constitution followed the British model, calling for a parliament (legislature), prime minister, and cabinet, as well as full voting rights for citizens.

Under Nyerere's leadership, the emerging nation focused on developing educational programs, increasing agricultural productivity, and fostering African unity. Equality was a particular concern of Nyerere's, not only for black Africans who were coming to political power but also for the Arab, European, and East Indian minorities. Nyerere also took a strong stand against apartheid—racial segregation—in the nation of South Africa. He appealed to all independent African nations to boycott, or refuse to buy, products from South Africa until apartheid policies were dropped.

# Independence for Tanganyika and Zanzibar

Tanganyika achieved self-government on May 1, 1961. The British governor still had the power to make limited decisions. Complete independence came in December of that year. Full independence meant that Tanganyika was freed entirely from colonial administration. Julius Nyerere became prime minister in the first independent government of Tanganyika. A National Assembly replaced the Legislative Council.

Nyerere encouraged European settlers to continue to live and work in independent Tanganyika. He did not want this class of wealthy and highly trained people to leave the new nation. Nevertheless, his goal was for African people to create solutions for the African continent.

Nyerere strongly supported the Organization for African Unity (OAU), which formed in 1963. The OAU brought together many of the newly independent nations of Africa. Together they attempted to solve disputes, to work for economic development, and to encourage cultural, scientific, and educational exchanges.

**Julius K. Nyerere (left)** met with U.S. president John F. Kennedy (right) in Washington, D.C., in July 1963—just months before Kennedy's assassination.

Zanzibar gained its independence from Great Britain on December 9, 1963. Independence intensified the problems on Zanzibar and the other islands, however. Two months later, Zanzibar was the scene of a bloody coup (government overthrow). The Afro-Shirazi Party leaders overthrew Sultan Seyyid Khalifa and the Arab ZNP leadership. ASP followers massacred thousands of Arabs and Indians. Abeid Amani Karume, head of the ASP, became the new leader of Zanzibar.

## Tanganyika and Zanzibar Unite

The governments of the world were surprised when Tanganyika and Zanzibar joined together in April 1964 to form the United Republic of Tanzania. But to people who knew East African history, the union was less surprising, since Zanzibar had long been the gateway to the East African mainland.

Nyerere realized that Zanzibar was in fragile condition because its life as a nation had begun with much tension and internal division. Tanganyika and Zanzibar allied into one nation to protect themselves and each other from the instability that threatened Zanzibar. TANU and the ASP already had political ties with each other. They joined to become the Chama Cha Mapinduzi (CCM), or the Revolutionary Party. Eventually, this single party ruled Tanzania and allowed no other parties to form. Only CCM candidates could run in elections.

Nyerere became the president of the new united republic. Zanzibar kept a lot of political independence. The president of Zanzibar, Karume, served also as vice president of Tanzania.

Karume's governing of Zanzibaris was harsh, especially toward the Arab minority. In 1972 Arab assassins murdered Karume. President Nyerere appointed Aboud Jumbe to succeed Karume as president of Zanzibar and as a vice president of Tanzania.

After achieving independence, Tanzania pursued a policy of African socialism. African Socialism stressed working together and sharing the fruits of labor. It also valued equality between men and women of all ethnic groups. The underlying idea is found in the movement's motto, *ujamaa*, meaning "togetherness" or "familyhood" in Swahili. Pursuing this vision, in the early 1970s, Nyerere's government forced huge numbers of rural people to move to farm villages that were run collectively. The government took control of big farms and factories. Production fell after these changes, and the plan led to economic disaster. The nation soon had to import food to feed its people.

## New Adversaries

Tanzania entered a period of conflict with Uganda, its neighbor to the north, in the 1970s. Uganda's president Milton Obote and his supporters had fled to Dar es Salaam after General Idi Amin had overthrown Obote. Amin installed himself as the country's dictator (ruler with absolute power). Nyerere was among the first outsiders to condemn Amin's brutal regime.

Although Nyerere wanted to avoid fighting Uganda directly, military conflict between the countries became more and more likely. Uganda occupied a portion of Tanzanian territory along their mutual border in 1978. In return, in 1979 Tanzania launched an invasion with twenty thousand troops. The Tanzanian forces, along with twelve hundred Ugandan exiles, captured Uganda's capital city of Kampala. Tanzania occupied a large portion of Uganda until 1981, when elections were held and Obote resumed the presidency.

Under Nyerere's leadership, Tanzania also supported independence movements in Angola, Mozambique, and Southern Rhodesia (modern Zimbabwe). Tanzania actively spoke out against apartheid and helped the outlawed African National Congress of South Africa.

In a gesture of reconciliation at the border between their nations, Tanzanian army leader **Yusuf Himidi** *(center left)* **clasps hands with Idi Amin,** president of Uganda in the early 1980s.

Tanzania faced a new challenge in the early 1980s. HIV and AIDS began to spread in sub-Saharan Africa (south of the Sahara, the desert that covers much of North Africa). Tanzania's health and education systems lacked funds to fully combat the disease, which is transmitted through body fluids. AIDS began to cripple communities, killing working-age adults and leaving thousands of orphans.

## Gains and Losses

In 1985, at the age of sixty-three, Nyerere stepped down from the presidency. He remained influential in his party, the CCM. Nyerere selected Ali Hassan Mwinyi to be the next president. Known as a politician who focused on the practical, Mwinyi began to reform Nyerere's Socialist policies gradually. The economy started to grow, but mismanagement and corruption held back the country's growth.

Tanzania reformed its constitution in 1992 to allow for full democracy, with more than one political party. Nyerere's hopes for South Africa were finally realized in 1994. That year South Africa reformed its political system, peacefully bringing apartheid and white minority rule to an end.

In Tanzania's 1995 elections, more than one party's candidate ran for president for the first time. Citizens elected CCM's candidate Benjamin Mkapa as president.

Meanwhile, semiautonomous (partly self-ruled) Zanzibar elected its own president and legislature. International observers claimed that Zanzibar's 1995 elections were irregular, or unfair, and even violent. Reports said that government-hired thugs threatened or attacked people who supported the opposition. The conflicts stemmed partly from the Arab minority's ongoing efforts to control Zanzibar's economy and politics.

The 1990s saw the growth of al-Qaeda in the Middle East and parts of Africa with large Muslim populations. Al-Qaeda is a terrorist network that seeks to institute strict Islamic law in place of secular (nonreligious) governments. It also uses violent means to try to remove Western (American and European) influences from the Muslim world. Tanzania—where about one-third of the population is Muslim—has historically had good relations with the United States. On August 7, 1998, terrorists linked to al-Qaeda exploded a car bomb outside the U.S. Embassy in Dar es Salaam. The bomb killed eleven people. Tanzanians of all faiths condemned the attack. Afterward, the two countries began to work closely together on antiterrorism programs.

The nation mourned when Julius Nyerere died in October 1999. Although his economic policies had been disastrous, his passionate support of Africa and Africans had made him a hero to many people.

The burned wreckage of the **U.S. Embassy in Dar es Salaam** one day after a car bomb exploded outside the embassy on August 7, 1998

# The Twenty-first Century

African leaders of the Organization of African Unity, which Nyerere had supported, held a meeting in 2000. Together they agreed to replace the OAU with a new organization called the African Union (AU). Modeled on the successful European Union, the AU works to promote peace, security, and trade among its more than fifty member nations, including Tanzania.

President Mkapa's policies created economic growth and increased international support for Tanzania during his first five-year term. In 2000 he won his second term, with 72 percent of the vote. The same year, voters in Zanzibar elected as president Ahmani Abeid Karume, the son of Zanzibar's first president.

Elections in Zanzibar once again were irregular, however. For instance, officials did not deliver ballots on time to areas where the opposition to the government was strongest. The fraud led to an outbreak of violence in Zanzibar in January 2001. Clashes with the police killed more than twenty people. Tens of thousands of protesters marched in Dar es Salaam. Talks between the main political parties led to an agreement to work together for election reforms.

The year brought another hopeful development. A huge, new gold mine, Bulyanhulu, opened in the north, near Mwanza. With this, Tanzania became Africa's third-largest gold producer.

While mainland Tanzania has remained mostly peaceful, terrible violence has racked many of its neighbors. The Second Congo War (1998–2003) in the Democratic Republic of Congo (DRC), for instance, killed an estimated 3.5 million people. Burundi also ended its decade-long civil war in 2003. The government of Tanzania worked to promote the peace agreements that ended the wars. Ongoing conflict among rebel groups in the eastern DRC continues, however. Hundreds of thousands of refugees fleeing from conflicts in the DRC and other countries further burden Tanzania.

After ten years as president, Benjamin Mkapa retired in 2005. Fraud again marred elections in Zanzibar, where President Karume won a close race that year. Elections on the mainland were peaceful. Jakaya Kikwete of the CCM won the presidential race, with 80 percent of the vote. He

**Jakaya Kikwete**

promised to continue Mkapa's economic reforms and to create jobs. Kikwete supports farming improvements, new roads, schools, and the development of gold and diamond mines. To encourage more reforms, in 2006 the African Development Bank canceled more than $640 million that Tanzania owed the bank. The hardworking and popular president also travels around the country, speaking publicly about the need to practice safe sex to prevent the spread of AIDS.

Zanzibar faces ongoing ethnic tensions, but the union with the mainland has largely been successful. While Tanzania overall remains one of the world's poorest countries, its citizens support a stable, democratic government. Other countries are willing to work with such a government. Tanzania continues to develop economically, socially, and politically.

## Government

The constitution of the United Republic of Tanzania outlines the executive, legislative, and judicial branches of the union's government. Zanzibar has its own similar constitution and government. In both regions, all citizens of eighteen years and older are eligible to vote.

The executive branch is composed of a president and vice president, elected by voters. The president, in turn, selects cabinet ministers to serve as advisers to the government. The president also appoints a prime minister. Citizens of Zanzibar elect a president, who is responsible for matters that concern the island group. The presidents of both Zanzibar and the United Republic of Tanzania serve five-year terms and may run for a second term.

The legislature of the union consists of the National Assembly, or Bunge, Tanzania's unicameral (one-house) lawmaking body. The assembly enacts laws for the entire republic. Zanzibar's fifty-member House of Representatives makes laws just for Zanzibar. Voters on Zanzibar elect house members. Voters in all of Tanzania elect 232 of the National Assembly's 274 members. The president appoints 37 women members, and members of Zanzibar's House of Representatives hold 5 seats in the National Assembly. Members of both legislatures serve five-year terms.

The judicial branch is made up of the High Court, which holds regular sessions in all regions. The president appoints its twenty-nine judges. District and primary courts have limited jurisdiction. Appeals are made to higher courts. A chief justice and four judges serve on the Court of Appeals. The legal system is based on British common law. Islamic and traditional African codes also influence Tanzania's law.

The United Republic of Tanzania is divided into twenty-six regions for administrative purposes. Twenty-one regions are on the mainland, three are on Zanzibar Island, and two are on Pemba. Local authorities operate through 114 district councils.

## WOMEN IN POLITICS

Women politicians in Tanzania have steadily increased their presence in government. Between 1995 and 2005, the percentage of women in the legislature rose from 11 percent to 21 percent. In 2006 President Kikwete named women to key positions in his cabinet (group of government advisers) for the first time in Tanzania. Zakia Meghji became the finance minister. Kikwete appointed Asha-Rose Migiro to be the foreign minister. Both women had previously held less important posts.

Tanzanian foreign minister Asha-Rose Migiro addresses a meeting of the UN Security Council on September 21, 2006. Visit www.vgsbooks.com for links to information about government officials in Tanzania.

# THE PEOPLE

Tanzania counts a population of 39 million people. Tanzania's people are young—about 44 percent are younger than fifteen. More than one quarter of Tanzanian women give birth by the age of eighteen, and the average woman gives birth five or six times in her life. With Tanzania's large number of young women coming into childbearing years, the population will keep growing rapidly. The population is increasing at a yearly rate of 2.5 percent. Experts estimate that by 2025, the country's population will number almost 54 million people. The government views the birthrate as too high. It works to educate people about family planning.

Disease and lack of health care slow the rate of population growth and lower the average life span. The nation ranks in the top fifteen countries in the world for HIV/AIDS prevalence (rate of infection).

Tanzania's population density is an average of 104 people per square mile (40 per sq. km). This is about average for eastern Africa. The population is not evenly distributed. In very dry areas, the population is only 3 people per square mile (1 per sq. km). Densely populated

Zanzibar averages 347 people per square mile (134 per sq. km). About 32 percent of Tanzanians live in urban areas. Many rural residents lack adequate sanitation such as clean water and sewage systems.

## Ethnic Mixture

The nation hosts several cultures, and many members of Tanzania's ethnic groups intermarry. Though important, ethnic loyalties are not central to national life. Family ties, however, are significant. Families gather to commemorate births, marriages, and deaths, as well as to celebrate good harvests. The people of Tanzania are almost all African in ethnic origin. People of non-African heritage account for only 1 percent of the population.

The coastal countries of East Africa are the home of many cultural groups of Asian, European, and African origin. Bantu-speaking communities migrated into present-day Tanzania during the first millennium (one thousand years) A.D. Arabic-speaking peoples from the Persian

Gulf and Oman settled along the coast. Persian-speaking people came from Shiraz in modern Iran. Many of the newcomers intermarried with the Bantu-speaking peoples. Gradually, the Swahili culture and language emerged as a blend of these groups.

South Asian immigration—from India and Pakistan to the mainland—began at the beginning of the twentieth century. South Asian workers came to build railways from the coast to the interior. Descendants of these railway employees frequently became merchants, technicians, and financial managers. Thousands of Europeans came to Tanzania during the first half of the twentieth century and settled in the area's fertile lands. In modern times, some occupy positions in private business or work as civil servants in schools and government offices.

## ◉ African Ethnic Groups

The African population includes more than 120 ethnic groups and cultures. Many groups are quite small. About 68 percent of Tanzanians live in rural areas. Many of these rural people speak Swahili in addition to English and the tongue of their individual ethnic group.

The Chaga and Masai live near Mount Kilimanjaro, where the countryside is fertile and gets plenty of rainfall. The Chaga are of Bantu origin. They live in one of the most densely populated areas of Tanzania. Their coffee-growing farms thrive. Many Chaga are successful business and professional people.

The Masai inhabit a sparsely populated plain west of Kilimanjaro that extends northward into Kenya. This group, which calls itself People of the Cattle, is well known throughout the world. Their military strength won the respect of European explorers during the nineteenth century, and their land was rarely disturbed. Masai villages are often temporary, because the group moves on when their herds require fresh grazing land.

These schoolchildren wash their hands and faces in fresh, **safe drinking water** at their school in a village in northeastern Tanzania.

In the central highlands, the population remains small but stable in spite of the country's overall population increase. Here, the largest ethnic groups are the Sukuma and the Nyamwezi. The Sukuma are subsistence farmers (able to grow only enough to feed themselves and their families) and cotton producers. The Nyamwezi have become known as traders in addition to being small-scale farmers. Few rivers originate in the region's dry forests, and many crop-destroying insects thrive. Therefore, the population in the region is sparse. Most settlements consist of only a few houses. A large village may have as many as one hundred houses.

The Makonde people of the southeast are famous for their arts, including mask making. They were important traders in the 1700s and 1800s. In modern times, most Makonde are farmers who live in villages. The main crops they grow to sell are cashew nuts and sisal.

The coastal, Swahili-speaking people live in cities and villages on the mainland and on nearby islands. They represent a variety of ethnic backgrounds but are included in the statistics as African. Most Swahilis are followers of Islam, the religion founded by the prophet Muhammad in the Middle East during the seventh century. Other groups came to the coastal region from the African interior or from Asia and eventually blended into the Swahili culture.

## ▶ Languages

The Tanzanian government adopted Swahili, or Kiswahili, a mixture of Arabic and Bantu, as its official language in 1967. Bantu words represent about two-thirds of the Swahili vocabulary. Most of the remaining one-third are of Arabic origin. Some German and English words entered Swahili in the twentieth century. For example, *shule* is the Swahili word for "school." It is nearly the same as the German word *schule*. *Motakaa* is the equivalent of "motor car" in English. Persian, Hindi (an Indian language), and Turkish also contributed to Swahili.

Tanzanians highly value politeness and generosity. They consider obscene language and harsh words to be unacceptable. Despite their social graces, they do not usually say "please" and "thank you." Bantu languages do not have native words for these terms. Instead, Tanzanians sometimes use Arabic-based Swahili terms. *Tafadhali* means "please," and *asante* means "thank you." However, Tanzanians are more likely to repay a favor with a good deed rather than with words.

Originally written in Arabic, modern Swahili employs the Latin alphabet used to write English. Arabic characters are used only for ceremonial documents. As a spoken language, Swahili spread along the trade routes. Millions of people living as far west as the Democratic Republic of Congo and as far south as Zambia use Swahili as a form of communication.

Some ethnic groups in northern Tanzania, near Arusha, speak Nilotic languages. This family of languages is generally associated with the cattle-herding people who originated along the Nile River valley. A few thousand other Tanzanians speak a form of click-tongue language. Clicking the tongue is a distinctive characteristic of some of the major languages of southern Africa. Some Tanzanians also speak English, a leftover from British rule.

## Health

Tanzania made health care a top national priority after independence in 1964. Life expectancy rose from 38 to 52 years. Then AIDS began to devastate the country in the 1980s, and life expectancy fell to 45 years. Only 4 percent of the modern population lives to be more than 65 years old. Eastern Africans as a whole can expect to live an average of 47 years. In comparison, the life expectancy in Great Britain—a former colonial ruler—is 78 years.

Tanzania's government is striving to increase the number of physicians as well as the number of available hospital beds. Only 822 doctors

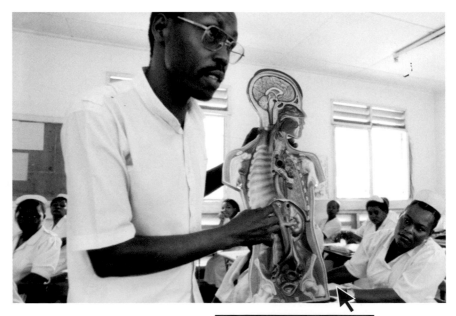

Nurses attend a health-care class at **Bagamoyo District Hospital.** This 150-bed facility serves a population of more than 230,000 residing in the district.

serve the entire country. Lack of funds limits what the government can do to improve health care. With most of the population living in rural areas, health care is expensive. Transportation costs are high, and electricity for refrigerating drugs is difficult to provide. Other countries assist Tanzania with money and advice. Religious groups provide a few well-run rural clinics.

Health-care workers distribute medicines and nutritional supplements to help fight the major diseases that challenge Tanzania—including tuberculosis (a lung disease), elephantiasis (a skin disease), smallpox, and malaria. Malaria racks the body with fevers and chills and can cause death. It is a leading killer of children in Africa. Many kinds of parasites spread illnesses that are major hazards to public health. Parasites attacking the intestines cause the disease schistosomiasis. The tsetse fly spreads trypanosomiasis (sleeping sickness) to humans and cattle in warm and wet regions of the country. The disease makes humans too weak and tired to work. Infected cattle slowly waste away.

Malnutrition, or the lack of enough nourishing food, is also common. It weakens people's resistance to disease. Furthermore, almost half of the population lacks access to clean water for drinking and washing. Waterborne diseases include dysentery (severe diarrhea), hepatitis A, and typhoid fever. Periodic cholera epidemics that kill hundreds of people also highlight the need for better water and sanitation systems.

Tanzanian women face a 1 in 10 chance of dying from causes related to childbearing during their lifetime. Only 36 percent of women give birth with the help of medically trained personnel. The country's infant mortality rate (IMR) is 68 deaths per 1,000 babies under one year old. This rate is lower than eastern Africa's average of 81 deaths per 1,000 babies. But it is far higher than the IMR of Great Britain (5.1 deaths per 1,000).

## FIGHTING MALARIA

Malaria threatens the health of Tanzanians, especially children. It is the leading cause of death in Zanzibar. Mosquitoes carry the parasites that cause malaria. The insects thrive in the islands' many swampy rice fields. Malaria-causing parasites have become resistant to medicines that used to treat the disease. In 2007 Dr. Theonest Mutabingwa of Tanzania tested a new drug called Lapdap on children with malaria. In the tests, the drug cured 93 percent of the children. Prevention, however, is cheaper than medicine. Health workers in Zanzibar have distributed almost 230,000 mosquito nets to hang over beds. The nets are treated with chemicals that kill mosquitoes.

Tanzania suffers with one of the highest rates of HIV/AIDS infection in the world. The medicines that help people with AIDS are generally not affordable. However, the government's active efforts to teach prevention methods—such as the use of condoms to prevent exchange of body fluids—has had some success. The HIV/AIDS prevalence of 6.5 percent of adults in 2007 is slightly lower than the 6.6 percent rate of infection in 2003. It is slowly falling to match the average prevalence of 6.1 percent for sub-Saharan Africa. International programs—such as the Global Fund to Fight AIDS, Tuberculosis, and Malaria—are important partners to the government's efforts to improve health care.

## Education

Education is one of the biggest priorities for Tanzania's government. Julius Nyerere emphasized education from the nation's very beginning. By the 1980s, Tanzania had one of Africa's highest rates of literacy, or people who could read and write. President Kikwete continues the emphasis on schooling for all Tanzanians.

The law requires children to attend seven years of primary school, and 82 percent of children enroll. The government stopped charging school fees for primary students in 2002. Primary schools offer instruction in history, geography, mathematics, health education, physical education, and science. Classes are conducted in Swahili, as well as in English. Secondary schools charge fees. Only 6 percent of children attend secondary schools.

Tanzania's overall literacy rate is 78 percent. Among young people, the rate is higher: 94 percent of young men and 89 percent of young women can read and write. The difference between the sexes reflects the lower number of girls who go to school. Families often keep girls home to work. About half of Tanzania's women have completed fifth grade.

**President Kikwete actively encourages Tanzanian girls to stay in school. He speaks publicly around the country, telling them to seek career opportunities, not babies.**

The country has one university, at Dar es Salaam. It offers courses in engineering, education, medicine, business, agriculture, and forestry. One agricultural college and nine other institutions offer higher education in the nation. The Institute of Kiswahili Research, for instance, provides opportunities for scholars of language and literature to explore the history of Tanzania's peoples. Forty-two teacher-training colleges, as well as many secondary and technical schools, also operate in Tanzania.

These boys take part in a tug-of-war on sports day at a <mark>state school</mark> in central Tanzania.

Visit www.vgsbooks.com for links to learn more about education, health, and housing in Tanzania.

##  Housing and Clothing

Urban Tanzanians live in modern apartment buildings and houses. Rural Tanzanians live in villages where often everyone is related to everyone else. Their homes are a variety of structures. A common housebuilding technique is to use wooden poles or branches to form a basic structure. The builders then fill the framework with wet clay. Sun-baked clay bricks are another common building material. The Waarusha people live in round wooden houses with grass thatch roofs. Masai women construct their families' homes from clay they make out of cattle dung mixed with mud. They apply this clay to walls they weave from branches and sticks.

Tanzanians who live in cities usually wear modest Western-style clothing. Men wear shirts and trousers. Only boys wear shorts, which are considered too informal and revealing for adults. Tanzania imports a large amount of used clothing from the United States, Europe, and Asia. In the countryside, where most Tanzanians live, traditional clothing is more common. Men may wear a long, cotton robe decorated with embroidery, called a *kanzu*. Women often wear blouses and wraparound skirts of colorful, printed cotton cloths called *kangas*. Different ethnic groups wear different styles. The Masai, for instance, wear togalike draped or knotted robes made of soft leather or red cloth.

# Cultural Life

With its background of many people from many places, Tanzania's culture is a colorful fusion of diverse influences. Incredible contrasts and inventions arose as Arab kingdoms on the islands mingled with native peoples of the interior. This mingling resulted in the dynamic blend of old and new found in Swahili culture. The nation's official language is the offspring of such meetings. Music also promotes lively meetings. Taraab music is popular on the coast, while the rhythms of Congo jazz show the influence of Africa's interior.

## Religion

Tanzania has a long history of African religions, Islam, and Christianity. Of Tanzanians, 30 percent hold Christian beliefs and 35 percent are of the Islamic faith. About 35 percent follow traditional African beliefs. The very small number of Tanzanians of southern Asian ancestry mostly follow the Hindu or Sikh religions.

Traditional African religions include a belief in a supreme being, a

reverence for one's ancestors, and a recognition of the connection between nature and spirit. The belief that spirit inhabits natural beings, objects, and events is sometimes called animism. In Tanzania, animist beliefs and practices often mix with Christian or Islamic ones. Villagers may attend Christian church services and also consult a traditional faith healer, who contacts spirits to cure ills.

On the islands, 99 percent of the people are Muslims. Arabs first brought the Islamic religion to Zanzibar. The prophet (spiritual spokesperson) Muhammad founded the religion on the Arabian Peninsula in the seventh century. The faith shares common roots with Judaism and Christianity, which also arose in the Middle East. Muslims believe that Allah (Arabic for "God") revealed his messages through the angel Gabriel to his chosen prophet Muhammad. Allah's words are recorded in the Quran, the holy book of Islam. Muslims strive to follow the main duties of Islam, known as the Five Pillars of Islam. They consist of declaring faith in God and his prophet

Muhammad, praying five times a day, giving to charity, fasting during the holy month of Ramadan, and making a pilgrimage (religious journey) to the holy city of Mecca, Saudi Arabia, if possible.

On the mainland, Roman Catholics make up the largest Christian denomination, with 18 percent of the population. The Portuguese first introduced the Catholic faith. Anglicans follow a branch of Christianity founded in Great Britain. The Lutheran faith has its roots in Germany. Both sects and other Protestant (non-Catholic Christian) religions are heavily represented in Tanzania's Christian population.

Tanzania has no state religion, and the government emphasizes tolerance among different religions. For instance, while Christian marriages are monogamous (allowing one spouse per person), Tanzanian law allows Muslim men and men who follow traditional African ways to have up to four wives at a time. Polygyny (allowing more than one wife) is more common among people who live in rural areas.

## Music and Dance

Music and dance have long been part of Tanzanian life, whether in songs and rhythms that accompany farming and other everyday activities or religious songs of praise. Traditional musical instruments include the marimba, or a xylophone. The thumb piano is also a traditional Tanzanian instrument. It consists of metal strips of varying lengths, which players pluck with their fingers (not just their thumbs). *Kayamba* shakers contain kernels of grain. *Siwa* are horns. Tambourines called *tari* and drums called *ngoma* come in many different sizes and styles.

*Taarab* music is a lively musical form that blends a rhythmic pre-Islamic style with Islamic melody. It is an important part of the social life of the islands and coast. Modern taarab bands such as Melody and Muungano play danceable taarab on keyboards.

Reported to be between 93 and 113 years of age, Tanzania's taarab music star Bi Fatuma Binti Baraka, popularly known as **Bi Kidude,** performs in Nairobi, Kenya. Her life is the subject of *As Old as My Tongue* (2006), a documentary film.

**Barabaig women dance at a wedding celebration.** This tiny ethnic group of the Great Rift Valley is a traditional enemy of the better-known Masai. For links to information on the different ethnic groups of Tanzania, visit www.vgsbooks.com.

Music from the Democratic Republic of Congo has been a major influence on its neighbors. Congolese musicians created upbeat, danceable Congo jazz, also called Congo rumba, in the 1960s. Remmy Ongala came to Tanzania from Zaire (Congo/DRC) in the late 1970s. He became a major force in Tanzanian music. Sometimes called the Bob Marley of Tanzania (after the reggae superstar of Jamaica), Ongala sings in Swahili about modern issues such as AIDS and poverty.

Tanzanian bands such as Twanga Pepeta build on Congolese and other influences. They create their own modern styles, such as Bongo Flava, which incorporates a wide range of melodies and beats. Bands play dance music in nightclubs and tour the country. Radio stations feature the latest popular Tanzanian musicians. These include Cool James, Juma Nature, Lady J. D., Professor Jay, and many others.

Traditional African dance is linked to religious rituals as well as special occasions and day-to-day activities. Drums provide the heartbeat of the dance. In fact, dance is called ngoma in Swahili, after the drums. In religious ceremonies, some dancers communicate with spirits. They express prayer and praise through rhythm and movement. The Makonde people in the southeast use masked dancers as part of the ceremonies for boys and girls coming of age.

**Ancient rock art** in Tanzania features an elephant. A Masai girl models fine examples of her ethnic group's **traditional jewelry.**

## ◉ Visual Arts

Ancient rock art found at several sites in Tanzania is more than three thousand years old. No one knows who made these images on rock walls. Using paints of mineral and animal fats, the artists portrayed people hunting and making music. They also painted animals such as antelope, giraffes, and elephants.

In modern times, Tanzanian traditional arts include carvings made of ebony wood and ivory. The carvings may convey traditional religious themes, capture the beauty of nature, or express Tanzanian humor. Roberto Jacobo is a well-known sculptor who carves interconnected figures from a single piece of wood. Basket makers decorate their woven baskets with complex geometric designs. The Masai are known for their beaded neck collars and other beaded jewelry. Arab influence in Zanzibar is evident in the fancy door carvings. Patterns of flowers, fruits, and fish cover these wooden doors.

Find more examples and information about art, music, and dance in Tanzania by visiting www.vgsbooks.com for links.

Some Tanzanian groups have traditionally practiced body arts, or body decoration. This art form includes elaborate hair styles and tattoos. People scar their skins in patterns as signs of beauty and elegance. Body painting with powdered minerals such as red yellow ochre makes bodies gleam. Some body-art practices, such as filing teeth to sharp points, have mostly disappeared in modern times.

In the twentieth century, Tingatinga paintings became popular in Tanzania. The art form is named after Edward Said Tingatinga (1937–1972). He painted scenes of local life and fanciful animals while he worked on building sites. When his brightly colored paintings became popular, he taught others to paint too. Modern artists continue to paint in his style, which employs tiny dots of paint.

## Literature

Tanzanians have a rich and deep tradition of oral, or spoken, literature. Storytellers have passed down their history, beliefs, folktales, and verse through the generations. Arab traders introduced the written Arabic language. Historians have reconstructed some of Tanzania's history from the written records of early Arab traders.

Because the people of Tanzania did not share a national language until after independence, the nation's written literature was slow to develop. Shaaban Robert (1909–1962) was one of Tanzania's most influential writers. He supported the development of writing in modern Swahili. His works include poetry and an autobiography. He also published collections of traditional African folktales and verse. Other writers in Swahili include Shafi Adam Shafi and short-story writer Joseph Mbele. Ebrahim Hussein is known for his plays. President Julius Nyerere wrote books about political issues. *Freedom & Development, Uhuru Na Maendeleo* (1974) is a collection of his essays.

*Popobawa* means "bat-wing" in Swahili. It is the name of a modern evil spirit of the sort found in the traditional Tanzanian storytelling. Residents of the island of Pemba first reported attacks by a Popobawa in 1995. They said that the smelly, sharp-clawed spirit mostly attacks men in their beds at night. Panic spread to coastal cities. Some Tanzanians who believed the stories used charms or sacrificed goats to keep the spirit away. Some men began to sleep outside. In 2007 reports from Dar es Salaam claiming a Popobawa was active once again renewed the hysteria.

People from other countries have also written about Tanzania. One of the most well-known stories is *The Snows of Kilimanjaro* (1939) by American writer Ernest Hemingway. West Indian-born Shiva Naipaul's *North of South—An African Journey* (1979) presents life in Tanzania in the 1970s.

Many modern Tanzanian authors write in English. Peter Palangyo's novel *Dying in the Sun* is about a young man who comes to accept his place with his rural family. M. J. Vassanji's fiction about Tanzania includes *The Book of Secrets* (1995).

Abdulrazak Gurnah is an English-language novelist from Zanzibar Island. He teaches literature in Great Britain. His fourth novel, *Paradise*, was published in 1994 to great acclaim. It is about a boy growing up in Tanganyika during World War I. *Desertion* (2005) begins in Zanzibar in 1899, with a love affair between a European man and an Indian woman. It reflects a common theme in Gurnah's novels—the condition of people being out of place or dealing with differences.

## Media

To promote Swahili as a unifying language, government-run Radio Tanzania began broadcasting in Swahili after independence. President Nyerere encouraged all Tanzanians to buy radios. They remain a main source of news and entertainment.

The small, state-controlled media developed quickly in the 1990s, when multiple political parties came on the scene. Lack of funds limits its growth, but dozens of radio stations serve the country. Tanzanians often get their news from international radio stations, including the BBC (British Broadcasting Corporation) and the Voice of America.

**Television came late to Tanzania. President Nyerere was against it because he thought it was luxury that would increase the gap between rich and poor people. State-run TV began in 2001.**

Most newspapers in Tanzania are written in Swahili. The government-owned *Daily News* is the country's oldest newspaper.

The mainland and Zanzibar follow different media rules. The international media-rights organization Reporters without Borders declares that Zanzibar allows no freedom of the press. The government of Zanzibar controls radio and television stations. It forbids private broadcasts or newspapers, although people on the islands can get stations and newspapers from the mainland.

A **soccer (football) player on the Zanzibar team** *(right)* kicks the ball away from a Cyprus player. The teams are taking part in the Alternative World Cup finals, the Federation of International Football Independents (FIFI) Wild Cup. Cyprus won this championship match, played on June 3, 2006, in Hamburg, Germany.

## Sports and Recreation

Soccer, track-and-field sports, and boxing are popular among Tanzanians. Volleyball is a favorite sport among girls. Visitors and well-off Tanzanians enjoy diving and other water sports at the nation's beautiful beaches.

The country has produced several world-class runners. Banuelia Mrashani won the Tokyo International Women's Marathon in 2002, when she was twenty-five. (Marathon races are 26.2 miles, or 42.1 kilometers, long.) Her time of 2:24:59 (hours: minutes: seconds) set a new record for the race. Her brother Simon Mrashani is also a runner. The two held the brother-sister record for the famous Boston Marathon until 2007. Samuel Mwera specializes in the men's 800 meter (2,625 feet) race. In 2005 he ran his personal best 800 meters in 1 minute 45.28 seconds. Mwera competed in the 2004 Summer Olympic Games in Athens, Greece. Restituta Joseph is a runner who competed in the women's 5,000 meters (16,404 feet) race at the 2004 Olympics.

During leisure time, Tanzanians love to socialize with family and friends. Tanzanians value hospitality, and they warmly welcome unannounced social visits. Men enjoy a version of a board game played all over Africa, called *bao* in Tanzania. Two players try to capture each other's counters—usually pebbles or seeds. The game is over when one player has captured all the other's counters.

## THE UHURU TORCH RACE

**The Uhuru (Freedom) Torch was lit for the first time on top of Mount Kilimanjaro after independence in 1961. It made real the symbolic words of Julius Nyerere, who had said that Tanzania would light a torch on top of Mount Kilimanjaro for unity, prosperity, security, and hope. The Uhuru Torch Race is held yearly. Each year on May 31, the torch is lit at a different important place. Runners carry the torch through the country for 147 days, ending on October 14, the date of Nyerere's death in 1999.**

## ⊙ Holidays

Tanzania's calendar of national secular holidays begins with New Year (January 1). Union Day (April 26) celebrates the 1964 union of Tanganyika and Zanzibar. Workers' Day, or Labor Day, falls on May 1. Saba Saba, which means "seven seven," on July 7 (7/7), marks the International Trade Fair. Farmers gather to sell their bounty of crops on Farmers' Day (August 8). October 14 honors the nation's first president with Mwalimu (Teacher) Nyerere Day and the climax of the Uhuru Torch Race. Independence Day on December 9 marks Tanganyika's 1961 independence from British rule. Local festivals throughout the year celebrate harvest and other events with feasting, singing, and dancing.

Tanzanians also respect Christian and Islamic holidays. National holidays in Tanzania include Christmas Day (December 25) and the day after, called Boxing Day. Christians celebrate Easter in March or April. A lunar (moon-based) calendar sets the dates of Islamic holy days celebrated as national holidays. Because the lunar calendar is eleven days shorter than the solar calendar in everyday use, the holidays' dates change from year to year. The month of Ramadan is a time of fasting (going without food or drink) from dawn until sunset. In the evenings, people gather to break their fast together. At the end of the month, Muslims celebrate Eid al-Fitr with three days of feasting. Muslims also celebrate Moulid (Muhammad's birthday) and Eid al-Kabir (the Feast of the Sacrifice) at the end of the annual pilgrimage to Mecca.

## ⊙ Food

Tanzanians generally grow their own food or shop for it daily in markets. Markets sell a variety of fruits and vegetables, mounds of colorful spices, meats, freshly caught fish, and even live chickens and pigeons. Islam forbids Muslims to eat pork or drink alcohol, but non-Muslims enjoy both.

Like most sub-Saharan Africans, Tanzanians generally cannot afford to eat much meat. Their diet is heavy on starches. The staples, or main foods, are cassava (a starchy root), cornmeal, bananas, and rice. Bananas are mashed or cooked in stews with vegetables or meat. *Ugali* is thick cornmeal porridge. With their fingers, diners dip a starch—often ugali rolled into balls—into a flavorful stew of vegetables and sometimes meat. Peanuts often add flavor and protein to dishes.

Food throughout much of East Africa is similar. For instance, Indian flat breads called chapati are popular throughout East Africa. Yet there are many variations. Cooking along the coasts and in Zanzibar has strong Arabic and Indian influences. Dishes often contain coconut. Coconut milk, a rich liquid made from coconut meat, is a popular ingredient in soups, curries, and desserts. Cooks mix different spices to make curry—a blend that flavors many dishes. Curry may include cumin, mustard seeds, black pepper, turmeric, cardamom, and cinnamon.

In the hot climate, diners enjoy fresh tropical fruits such as pineapples, mangoes, or papayas for dessert. Fruit drinks, called squashes, are popular in Tanzania. Coffee or tea may be served after a meal. Chai is Indian-style hot, milky tea brewed with honey or sugar and spices.

## PLANTAINS IN COCONUT MILK

This Swahili dish made with plantains, a kind of banana, goes well with any curry dish. If you can't find plantains, you can substitute hard, green bananas. If you like, serve this dish with chai. To make chai, boil 4 cups water. Add 4 tea bags of black tea, ½ tsp. cardamom, 1 tsp. cinnamon, and ½ cup sugar. Simmer on low heat for 10 minutes. Add 4 cups milk, and heat chai again. Serve hot.

4 plantains

½ teaspoon mild curry powder

½ teaspoon cinnamon

a few cloves, or a pinch of powdered cloves

⅛ teaspoon salt

1 can coconut milk

1. Peel plantains. Cut plantains into thick, round slices.
2. Mix spices together in a saucepan. On low heat, slowly stir coconut milk into spices until all is absorbed.
3. Add plantains. Simmer until plantains are tender, about 20 minutes. Add a little water if necessary.

Serves 4 to 6

# THE ECONOMY

Tanzania has historically been and largely remains an agricultural country. During the colonial period, the Germans and the British built fewer roads and railways in mainland Tanzania than they did in other areas of East Africa. They also developed less industry. Moreover, the mainland's export trade did not thrive as Zanzibar's did.

The newly independent government inherited these underdeveloped conditions in 1964. It set out to improve and modernize the country's economy. The first president, Julius Nyerere, called for self-reliance. His government set up new farm villages and nationalized (changed from private ownership to government control) factories, plantations, banks, and private companies. The World Bank (a United Nations agency) and sympathetic countries provided financial and technical aid to the new country. Nevertheless, Nyerere's programs failed. Inefficiency, corruption, resistance from farmers, and skyrocketing prices of imported oil in the 1970s brought the country to bankruptcy by the time Nyerere resigned in 1985.

Nyerere's successors raised productivity and attracted investment and loans from other countries. Gradually, control of the economy returned to private owners. Loans have left Tanzania carrying a heavy debt load, however.

Tanzania's economy is growing at an average annual rate of almost 6 percent. This rate shows Tanzania to be one of the best economic performers in sub-Saharan Africa. Tanzania's government and citizens are working along with international donors to modernize Tanzania. They face many challenges. Power supplies and transportation systems do not meet the nation's needs. A debt of almost $5 billion cripples the country's economy. Some international lenders have forgiven Tanzania's debts to help the country get on its feet.

Yet Tanzania is still one of the poorest countries in the world. The average yearly income per person is $730. About 90 percent of the population lives on less than $2 per day.

This **roadside store** in northeastern Tanzania brims with fresh bananas and plantains.

## Agriculture, Fishing, and Forestry

Agriculture, including farming, livestock raising, fishing, and forestry, provides about 43 percent of Tanzania's gross domestic product (GDP, the value of the goods and services produced by a country over one year). It accounts for 80 percent of the workforce and much of the nation's exports. Rough terrain and climate conditions, however, limit croplands to 4 percent of the country's land.

Tanzanians provide most of their own food. Most Tanzanian farms are small and are worked by hand with simple tools. Farmers grow rice, cassava, corn (called maize in Africa), sugarcane, and peanuts on small farms that dot the countryside. Bananas, mangoes, papayas, and pineapples are among the nation's many tropical fruits. Farmers also grow sweet potatoes, tomatoes, onions, and other vegetables. These products are not exported, however, because Tanzania needs them for food.

Significant changes, such as the introduction of chemical fertilizers and mechanization, modernized the agricultural methods used by Tanzanian farmers since the 1960s. As world oil prices rise, however, fertilizers and other petroleum-based products become too expensive for farmers.

The government of Tanzania encourages farmers to work together to develop cooperative farms. The government believes that cooperatives will increase agricultural output through groups cooperating to purchase seeds and fertilizers and to sell their produce.

Tanzanians raise cattle in regions where rainfall is scarce and where crops are difficult to grow. In traditional African communities, people consider cattle a measure of a family's wealth and prestige.

Tanzania has more than 17 million head of cattle. The nation's herd is the third-largest in Africa. Only farmers in Ethiopia and Sudan raise more cattle.

The most common breed of livestock is the humped zebu, a small, short-horned variety of cattle. Ranchers near Lake Victoria raise a long-horned breed called the ankole. In addition to cattle, Tanzanians commonly raise sheep, goats, and donkeys. Chickens are common in Tanzania. They are considered a special food and are often eaten at holiday time or on other special occasions.

Tanzania's waters are an important source of fish. Tilapia, Nile perch, and other freshwater fishes make up the main catches. Fishing crews catch almost 400,000 tons (360,000 metric tons) every year. The nation is working to increase the yield. Experts estimate that Tanzania's potential yield of fish could more than double.

**Spectacular freshwater tropical fish live in Lake Victoria. Tanzania exports many of the colorful species to aquariums all over the world.**

Woodlands and dense forest cover more than 13 percent of Tanzania. The trees are valuable as a raw export material. Generally, the forests are situated at high altitudes in northern and northeastern Tanzania, where rainfall is plentiful. Southwestern Tanzania also contains important areas of standing timber. Mangrove forests cover most of the coastal region. The principal timbers cut for commercial use are mahogany, cedar, blackwood, and camphorwood. Since 1920 the government has managed the forests and constantly improves their use and conservation.

## Main Export Crops

In addition to developing the farm economy to better feed the nation's people, Tanzania also strives to increase its production of cash crops. These crops, grown to sell, provide money essential for economic growth. The main countries that buy Tanzania's exports are China, Canada, England, India, the Netherlands, Japan, and Germany.

The main crops Tanzania sells abroad are sisal, cloves, coffee, cotton, cashew nuts, and tobacco. Other spices and tea are also major export crops. Tanzania also exports pyrethrum, an insecticide (bug killer) made from chrysanthemums. Farmers began raising flowers for export in the mid-1990s. Flower farms are near the Kilimanjaro airport, where they can be shipped to Europe.

Cotton grows along the coast and in the plateau regions up to 4,000 feet (1,219 m) above sea level, as well as in areas around Lake Victoria. Farmers grow almost all Tanzania's cotton on small farms. They sell it through cooperatives.

The rich coffee beans of Tanzania are popular in Europe, Asia, and the United States. One of Tanzania's most valuable cash crops, coffee beans grow mostly in the northern mountains. Many farmers have small holdings and sell their crop through the national coffee cooperative. Europeans and Asians own many of the northern coffee plantations. They hire Tanzanians to grow and harvest the crop.

Foreign investors also raise tea on large acreages. Grown mainly in the southern highlands and in the northeastern mountains near Tanga, the tea is marketed in London, England, and in Nairobi, Kenya.

## Zanzibar's Economy

Zanzibar, like the mainland, has mainly an agricultural economy. Cloves, cardamom, and other spices grown on the Indian Ocean islands are Tanzania's fourth-largest export. They are Zanzibar's main agricultural product. The islands of Zanzibar and Pemba have earned the nickname the Islands of Cloves because they produce the majority of the world's cloves and clove oil.

The clove industry in Zanzibar dates from the 1830s, when the island served as a base for Arab activity in East Africa. Sultan Seyyid Oman introduced the spice to the island. In less than seventy-five years, the clove plantations of Zanzibar were producing about three-fourths of the world's supply.

Cloves come from the dried flower bud of a tropical tree. Cooks around the world use them in the preparation of food. The spice is also an important ingredient in the production of cigarettes in southern Asia.

Merchants export many of Tanzania's cloves to that region.

Other Zanzibar exports include coconuts and copra. Copra, the dried meat of the coconut, is the source of coconut oil. It is an ingredient in making

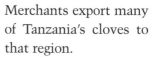

**Tourism to Tanzania's Indian Ocean islands is an important source of revenue. Visitors are drawn to these islands' beautiful beaches, warm waters, and historic sights.**

soap. The local government of Zanzibar has introduced a variety of other crops. For instance, it encourages growing rice for local use. Zanzibar also produced seashells, pottery, jewelry, rope, and mats.

## Services, Transportation, and Communication

The service sector offers public and private services rather than the production of goods. It includes jobs in tourism, government, health care, education, retail trade, transportation, and communications. The service sector accounts for 39 percent of Tanzania's GDP. It employs 17 percent of the nation's workforce.

Tourism is an important source of income for Tanzania. The country's attractions include Africa's highest mountain, Kilimanjaro, the Serengeti National Park and other wildlife-rich national parks, and the nation's beautiful islands. The Tanzania Tourist Board encourages and develops this sector of the economy. Ngorongoro Crater, Olduvai Gorge, Lake Victoria, and Lake Tanganyika are among the other destinations of many foreign visitors each year.

In Tanzania five motor vehicles are in use per 1,000 people. Workers in cities usually travel to and from work by foot, bicycle, or bus.

Tanzania's tourist industry objected in 2007 when Kenya's minister of tourism said that Mount Kilimanjaro was one of its country's top tourist attractions. In fact, the mountain is in Tanzania, about 12 miles (20 km) from the Kenyan border.

Bicycles are a popular and economical form of transportation throughout Tanzania.

**Workers lay asphalt** on a road near the city of Arusha.

Buses connect all the major cities and towns and serve most of the rural areas. Almost 50,000 miles (80,000 km) of roadways serve Tanzania. Only 45 miles (72 km) of the roads are paved.

Tanzania has 2,306 miles (3,711 km) of railways. The Tanzanian government—in cooperation with the Zambian government and China—completed a 1,116-mile-long (1,796 km) railway line in 1947. It links the copper-producing country of Zambia to the seaport of Dar es Salaam. The railroad is a vital overland connection.

Lakes Tanganyika, Victoria, and Nyasa are major trade routes for boat traffic with neighboring countries. Commercial boats cannot navigate Tanzania's rivers. Dar es Salaam, Mtwara, and Zanzibar City serve as the nation's major ports on the Indian Ocean.

Eleven of Tanzania's 124 airports have paved runways. International airlines serve the major cities. Smaller aircraft leave daily from Dar es Salaam for the national game parks and tourist centers.

Modern technology has revolutionized communications in Africa. In Tanzania—a country with only 150,000 landlines—more than 2 million people use cell phones. Because computers are expensive, fewer than 1 million people employ the Internet privately. But many users share connections at Internet cafés or at work.

# Industry and Imports

The industrial sector, including mining, accounts for 18 percent of Tanzania's GDP. It employs 3 percent of the workforce. Industrial development has been slow in Tanzania. The nation has lacked money to invest in industry since the colonial period. Poor roads and insufficient power supplies also have slowed development of the country's industrial wealth. The government seeks to establish new industries. It particularly welcomes private investments in small companies that will provide essential goods for Tanzanians.

Tanzania's industries mainly process agricultural goods. Factories produce sugar, beer, cigarettes, and sisal twine. The textile industry relies on cotton the nation produces. Textiles, clothing, and raw cotton are sold extensively abroad. Industries also produce cement, shoes, wood products, and fertilizer.

Tanzania imports more than it exports, which means it spends more abroad than it earns. It buys consumer goods, used clothing, machinery, transportation equipment, and medicines from other countries. It also relies on other countries for oil and raw materials for industry. Its main import suppliers are South Africa, China, India, Britain, Germany, the United Arab Emirates, Kenya, and the United States.

Tanzanian farmers produce cotton for direct export. Tanzania's cotton crop also supplies the nation's textile industries.

## Mining and Energy

Tanzania mines gold, gems, and industrial diamonds. Gold increased in importance after the 2002 opening of the large gold mine at Bulyanhulu. Tanzania is Africa's third-largest gold producer. Miners have been digging diamonds since 1940 in western Tanzania and around the port of Mwanza. Some of the diamonds are of gem quality. The rest are sold for industrial purposes. The earth's hardest mineral, diamonds are valuable in precision-cutting tools.

Secondary minerals mined in Tanzania include iron, salt, soda ash, limestone, tin, and mica (a thin, transparent metal). Other gemstones include tanzanite (a blue gemstone), rubies, and sapphires.

Tanzania gets most of its energy from dams on rivers, which produce hydroelectric power. Hydroelectricity provides 91 percent of the country's electricity. The nation produces no petroleum or natural gas yet. It must spend money to buy fuel from other countries. Companies are exploring for oil and natural gas deposits in Tanzania.

### TANZANIAN EXCLUSIVE

**Tanzanite is a blue gemstone. It exists only in Tanzania, southwest of Mount Kilimanjaro. However, smugglers illegally transport the precious stones into other countries where they will earn higher prices. The practice is so common that Kenya exports more tanzanite than Tanzania does. In 2002 the American Gem Trade Association made tanzanite an alternate birthstone (a gem that symbolizes the month of a person's birth) for December.**

A gemologist examines pieces of tanzanite under a special lamp.

Striking a balance between preserving the **beauty of natural waterfalls,** such as this one in east central Tanzania, and damming rivers to produce hydroelectricity will continue to challenge Tanzania in the future.

Visit www.vgsbooks.com for links to the latest news from Tanzania, a currency converter, and information about tourism and other aspects of this East African nation's economy.

 ## The Future

Tanzania faces many challenges, including high levels of poverty and AIDS. However, its government is working to improve the economy and the overall quality of life. Tanzania is politically stable in a region that has been marked by instability. International donors are willing to invest in such a country. It seems likely that Tanzania's economic growth and good relations with other countries will continue. One of President Nyere's early sayings was, "Independence is work." Tanzanians are committed to continuing the work of making their country one of Africa's success stories.

**CA. 2.3 MILLION B.C.**

Ancestors of modern humans live in Olduvai Gorge.

**CA. 10,000 B.C.**

Hunter-gatherers from western Africa migrate to present-day Tanzania.

**CA. 1000 B.C.** Different cattle-herding groups from the north enter mainland Tanzania.

**CA. A.D. 1** Bantu-speaking people from the northwest begin to move to the mainland. In the same era, Roman traders reach the coast of East Africa.

**CA. 700** Traders from the Arabian Peninsula begin arriving on the islands and coasts of present-day Tanzania. Gradually, they spread their religion, Islam, and their Arabic language, beginning the rise of the African-Arab Swahili culture.

**CA. 800** Arab traders dominate the large Indian Ocean trading business of African gold, ivory and other goods, and slaves. The ancestors of the Masai and the Luo move southward into Tanzania.

**CA. 1100** Traders and settlers arrive from Shiraz, Persia (modern Iran). Merchants from India also do business with Swahili traders.

**1498** Portuguese explorer Vasco da Gama visits Tanzania's coast. His reports spark eventual ongoing war between the Portuguese and Arabs for control of the East African coast.

**1650s** Arabs from Oman in southern Arabia take control of Zanzibar. Battle for control with the Portuguese continues.

**1698** The Arabs have driven the Portuguese from Tanzania for good. Zanzibar becomes part of the sultanate (kingdom) of Oman.

**1840** Sultan Seyyid Said moves his capital from Muscat, Oman, to Zanzibar. He encourages Indian migration and the use of slaves to develop clove plantations. In this decade, the first groups of European missionaries arrive in East Africa.

**1876** The British convince the sultan of Zanzibar to stop trading (but not to stop owning) slaves.

**1890** Germany gains control of German East Africa: present-day Rwanda, Burundi, and mainland Tanzania. The German East Africa Company harshly rules the colonies. Zanzibar remains under Arab rule.

**1905** The two-year Maji-Maji Revolt begins. For the first time, different African ethnic groups unite to fight for independence, but German troops put down the revolt.

**1911** Slavery comes to a final end in Zanzibar.

**1912** Warmer global temperatures begin to melt Mount Kilimanjaro's ice and snow cover.

1919    After World War I, the League of Nations places Tanganyika
        under British control.

1946    After World War II, the United Nations makes Tanganyika a trusteeship
        under British control.

1961    Tanganyika achieves self government. Tanganyika African National Union
        (TANU) leader Julius Nyerere becomes prime minister. The next year, he becomes
        president of the Tanganyikan republic.

1964    One year after Zanzibar becomes independent, the African majority of the islands
        overthrows the minority Arab ruling elite. Tanganyika and Zanzibar merge to become
        Tanzania, with Nyerere as president, and Zanzibar leader Abeid Amani Karume as vice
        president.

1977    The TANU and Zanzibar's Afro-Shirazi Party merge to become the CCM, the country's only
        legal party

1979    Tanzanian troops occupy Uganda's capital, Kampala. They help to overthrow the
        dictatorship of President Idi Amin.

1985    Nyerere retires. Zanzibar's president Ali Mwinyi succeeds him. AIDS is spreading through
        sub-Saharan Africa.

1995    Tanzanians elect Benjamin Mkapa as president in Tanzania's first multiparty election.

1999    Julius Nyerere dies.

2001    Protests erupt across the country after Tanzanian security forces shoot people who oppose
        the government in Zanzibar. The government agrees to election reforms. A new gold mine,
        Bulyanhulu, opens. State-run TV begins to broadcast.

2002    Tanzania's worst train disaster kills almost three hundred people when a high-speed
        passenger train loses power and rolls into a freight train.

2004    Restituta Joseph competes in the women's 5,000-meter (16,404 feet) race at the
        Summer Olympics in Athens, Greece.

2005    Scientists discover the kipunji—a previously unknown monkey species—in Tanzania's
        southern mountain forests. Jakaya Kikwete wins the presidential election.

2006    The African Development Bank cancels more than $640 million of Tanzania's debt.
        President Kikwete names two women to key government jobs.

2007    Tanzania's HIV/AIDS prevalence of 6.5 percent of adults reflects a slight
        reduction since 2003. President Kikwete supports education to prevent the
        spread of AIDS. A fishing crew catches a rare coelacanth off the coast of
        Zanzibar.

**COUNTRY NAME** United Republic of Tanzania

**AREA** 364,881 square miles (945,037 sq. km)

**MAIN LANDFORMS** Great Rift Valley, Western Rift Valley, Olduvai Gorge, Ngorongoro Crater, Mount Kilimanjaro, Uluguru Mountains, Zanzibar archipelago

**HIGHEST POINT** Mount Kilimanjaro, 19,340 feet (5,895 m)

**LOWEST POINT** floor of Lake Tanganyika, 2,300 feet (690 m) below sea level

**MAJOR RIVERS** Malagarasi, Moyowosi, Pangani, Rufiji, Ruvuma

**ANIMALS** antelope, baboons, chimpanzees, elephants, giraffes, hippopotamuses, hyenas, jackals, kipunji (highland mangabey), lions, monkeys, rhinoceroses, wildebeests (gnus), zebras, herons, flamingos, parrots, pelicans, sea turtles, starfish

**CAPITAL CITIES** Dodoma

**OTHER MAJOR CITIES** Dar es Salaam, Mwanza, Arusha, Zanzibar City, Tanga

**OFFICIAL LANGUAGE** Swahili (also called Kiswahili)

**MONETARY UNITY** Tanzania shilling. 1 Tanzania shilling = 100 cents

## CURRENCY

The unit of currency is the Tanzania shilling (abbreviated TShs). The shilling is divided into 100 cents. Shillings come in colorful notes (paper money) of 5, 10, 20, 50, 100, 200, 1,000, 5,000, and 10,000 denominations. Coins are gold or silver colored. They come in denominations of 5, 10, 20, and 50 cents. Shilling coins are in denominations of 1, 5, 10, 20, 50, 100, and 200 shillings. The money features Tanzanian wildlife, such as the wildebeest; cultural images, such as the Uhuru torch; and portraits of famous people such as President Julius Nyerere, who is considered the father of independence.

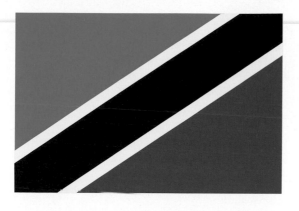

The center black stripe of Tanzania's flag runs on a slant, rising from the left (flag-pole side) up to the right. Two narrower gold stripes run along either side of the black stripe. They divide the top triangle, which is green, and the bottom triangle, which is blue. The flag's colors are symbolic. Black symbolizes the country's people. Green stands for its land. Blue is the color of its waters, and gold represents its mineral wealth.

Tanzania was the first African nation to use the popular African song "Mungu Ibariki Afrika" (God Bless Africa) as its anthem. South Africa and Zambia also use variations on the song. Tanganyika adopted it at its independence in 1961. The nation kept the anthem after union with Zanzibar in 1964. Enoch Mankayi Sontonga wrote the music. The words come from tradition. Below is the first verse and chorus in the original Swahili and in English.

### "Mungu Ibariki Afrika" (God Bless Africa)

| Swahili | English Translation |
|---|---|
| Mungu Ibariki Afrika, | God Bless Africa, |
| Wabariki viongozi wake. | Bless its leaders. |
| Hekima, umoja na amani | Let wisdom, unity, and |
| Hizi ni ngao zetu | Peace be the shield of |
| Afrika na watu wake. | Africa and its people. |
| **Chorus:** | **Chorus:** |
| Ibariki, Afrika | Bless Africa, |
| Ibariki, Afrika | Bless Africa, |
| Tubaki, watoto wa Afrika. | Bless the children of Africa. |

Visit www.vgsbooks.com for links to hear Tanzania's national anthem, "Mungu Ibariki Afrika."

**RESTITUTA JOSEPH** (b. 1971) Born in Singida, Joseph is a long-distance runner. She ran her personal best time of 2:43:52 in the marathon (a 26.2 miles, or 42.1 kilometer, race) in 2001. She competed in the women's 5,000 meters (16,404 feet) race at the 2004 Summer Olympics in Athens, Greece, but did not win a medal.

**JAKAYA MRISHO KIKWETE** (b. 1950) Born in Msoga, Kikwete was elected to be Tanzania's president in December 2005. His father worked for the British colonial government, and his grandfather was a chief. Kikwete studied economics at the University of Dar es Salaam, and he went on to serve his country in the military and as a foreign minister. He worked with Tanzania's founding president, Julius Nyerere. Kikwete represents the ruling CCM party, which has controlled Tanzania since independence. Upon election, he promised to continue President Benjamin Mkapa's economic reforms and to create jobs and reduce poverty. Kikwete, popularly known as JK, likes sports and supports the national basketball team.

**FREDDIE MERCURY (FAROOKH BULSARA)** (1946–1991) One of Zanzibar's most famous exports was Freddie Mercury. He was a songwriter and the lead singer of the British glam-rock band Queen. Born Farookh Bulsara in Zanzibar, he and his Shirazi family moved to London, England, when he was seventeen. But Mercury never forgot his roots. In his smash hit song "Bohemian Rhapsody," for instance, Mercury used the Swahili term *bismillah*, which means "in the name of God." His death from AIDS in 1991 greatly increased worldwide awareness of the disease.

**ASHA-ROSE MIGIRO** (b. 1955) Born in Tanzania, Migiro earned her law degree in Germany. She became the head of the law faculty at the University of Dar es Salaam. A champion of human rights, she became the first black woman and first African to serve as deputy secretary general of the United Nations. Her appointment came as Tanzania took over the presidency of the UN Security Council. In her role, she presided over the council's meetings in New York City. In 2006 President Kikwete named Migiro as Tanzania's first woman foreign minister. Some people started to call her the Condoleezza Rice of Tanzania, referring to the U.S. secretary of state.

**BENJAMIN MKAPA** (b. 1938) Mkapa retired in 2005, after serving two terms as Tanzania's president. Born in the historic coastal town of Bagamoyo, Mkapa showed an interest in politics even as a boy. As president, he led the drive to reform the country's economy. Under his leadership, inflation (price rises) lessened, the economy grew, and Tanzania's foreign debt shrank. While international lenders were pleased, critics pointed out that most Tanzanians remained poor.

## JULIUS KAMBARAGE NYERERE (1922–1999) Born in Tanganyika to a local Zanaki chief, Nyerere became Tanzania's first president in 1964. In college he translated plays by William Shakespeare into Swahili, among other achievements. He became a schoolteacher, but he quit to peacefully lead Tanganyika to independence in 1961. Nyerere wanted his country to avoid the dangers he saw in greed and corruption. His idea of a solution was ujamaa (familyhood). He based his vision for Tanzania on traditional African societies, in which everyone worked together. His ideals led to economic decline, which he later took responsibility for. However, he did succeed in steering a unified Tanzania clear of the ethnic strife and government corruption that plagued many other African nations after independence. Nyerere served as president for twenty-one years before retiring in 1985. Tanzanians always called their well-respected first president Mwalimu, which means "teacher" in Swahili.

## SHAABAN ROBERT (1909–1962) Shaaban Robert was one of modern Tanzania's most important writers. Born in Vibamba, he received only a few years of schooling, but he came to be known as the father of Swahili literature. He worked for the colonial government but joined TANU to support the struggle for independence from foreign rule. In his poems, prose, and essays, he promoted the use of the Swahili language. He also was a champion for human rights, supporting equal rights for women and men and for all races and religions.

## JUDITH WAMBURA (b. 1979) Born in Tanzania, Judith Wambura is a top-selling musician known as Lady J. D., or Jaydee. She began her performing career as a gospel singer before she began to perform dance music. Along with other Bongo Flava musicians, she is known for blending East African styles popular in the 1970s (such as Congo rumba) with contemporary hip-hop. She has said that she finds the deep human themes in the works of past musicians. She is also an innovative remixer. She released her fourth album, *Shukrani*, in 2007.

## EDINA YAHANA (b. 1981) Yahana was born in the village of Kambai in mountainous northeastern Tanzania. By the time she was thirteen, deforestation had reduced much of the lush rain forest near her home. As a teen, Yahana took a job with the Tanzania Forest Conservation Group (TFCG). The group hired villagers to raise saplings (young trees) to replace forest trees. Yahana was so successful, TFCG hired her to be an assistant forester. She travels in rural areas teaching villagers ways to help protect the environment, including growing and planting young trees. Because people rely on forest wood for fuel, she also teaches practical ways to use less firewood, such as how to build mud ovens, which require less fuel than open fires. Yahana also helps villagers implement income-earning programs, including fish-farming projects.

**DAR ES SALAAM** is Tanzania's largest city and main port. It sits in a calm bay off the Indian Ocean coast. Visitors enjoy the National Museum, the Village Museum, the Botanical Gardens, and walking along the historic waterfront. Lively and colorful markets thrive along with modern restaurants and shops. German and British colonial architecture remains, including Saint Joseph's Cathedral and the old State House. Just north of the city lies the Bongoyo Island Marine Reserve. The reserve offers beautiful beaches and good sites for divers.

**LAKE VICTORIA** is Africa's largest lake. The area's gently sloping hills lead to sparkling blue waters, offering excellent opportunities for boating and fishing trips, hikes, and bird-watching. Tanzania's area includes the Rubondo Island National Park.

**MOUNT KILIMANJARO** is the highest and most famous mountain in Africa. Climbing to the summit takes an average of five days. The slow pace is necessary to protect hikers from altitude sickness—dizziness and nausea or worse that strikes people unused to the low oxygen level at high altitudes. Hikers don't need ropes or climbing equipment to make it to the top. The route passes through thick forests and grasslands to brilliant white fields of ice and snow. From the top, the Masai Steppe, the Northern Highlands, and Kenya are visible.

**NGORONGORO CONSERVATION AREA** is home to the famous Ngorongoro Crater and the Olduvai Gorge, where scientists discovered the remains of a 1.8 million-year-old skeleton of a human ancestor. Lions and large herds of zebra and wildebeest roam the crater's grasslands, while Masai people herd their animals on the highland slopes. Visitors can hike or drive through this beautiful part of Tanzania.

**SERENGETI NATIONAL PARK** is Africa's most famous national park. Its vast grasslands present the classic image of wild Africa. The range of familiar African wildlife—lions, elephants, giraffes, zebras, and more—is present in awe-inspiring numbers. Visitors can witness the annual migration of a million wildebeest, after the twice-yearly rains. Tour operators offer a range of safaris, from jeep tours to hot-air ballooning over the plains.

**ZANZIBAR ISLAND** offers some of the best beaches in the world. The west coast's old port city, called Stone Town, remains unchanged. Visitors can walk through a maze of streets winding between the sultan's palace, the Portuguese fort, and merchants' houses. Caves where slaves were held are visible at low tide at the nearby beaches of Mangapwani. Tours of the island's famous working plantations offer the chance to see the cultivation of cloves and other spices. The Menai Bay Conservation Area protects sea turtle's breeding grounds on the south coast. Zanzibar City hosts the annual Zanzibar International Film Festival.

**animism:** a religious practice of spirit worship. Practitioners believe spirit (conscious life) inhabits all living and nonliving natural objects, natural events (such as lightning), and human ancestors.

**Bantu:** a family of languages spoken in central and southern Africa

**colony:** a territory controlled by a foreign nation and partially inhabited by settlers from that foreign land

**coup:** the sudden, often violent, overthrow of a government

**dictator:** a leader who rules with absolute power, often through oppressive and violent means

**equator:** an imaginary circle around the earth that is halfway between the North Pole and the South Pole. The equator divides the Northern Hemisphere and the Southern Hemisphere. The climate near the equator is the world's hottest.

**gross domestic product (GDP):** the value of the goods and services produced by a country over a period of time, usually one year

**literacy:** the ability to read and write a basic sentence

**poaching:** the catching or killing of animals illegally

**polygyny:** the practice of a husband having more than one wife at once, common in traditional sub-Saharan African societies and in Islam

**Shirazi:** from or characteristic of Shiraz, a part of Persia (present-day Iran). Shirazi people in Tanzania often have some African or Arab heritage too.

**sub-Saharan Africa:** the part of the African continent that is south of the Sahara, the desert that covers much of North Africa. In 2008 the region included forty-eight nations.

**subsistence farmer:** a farmer able to grow just enough to feed the family, with no surplus food left over to sell

**sultan:** a Muslim ruler. A sultanate is the power of the sultan or the region the sultan controls.

**tropical rain forest:** a warm, humid, and thick woodland that lies in regions near the equator, where rain is plentiful and temperatures are warm year-round

**the West:** the industrialized, non-Communist nations west of Asia, including the nations of Europe and the Americas

*Africa South of the Sahara.* **London: Routledge, 2007.**
This volume is part of the annual Europa Regional Surveys of the World series. Its long, in-depth article on Tanzania covers the country's recent history, economy, and government. It also offers a wealth of statistics on population, employment, trade, and more. A short directory of offices and organizations is included.

**Ali-Dinar, Ali B., ed. "Tanzania Page." Africa Studies Center. University of Pennsylvania. 2007.**
http://www.africa.upenn.edu/Country_Specific/Tanzania.html (September 2007).
This site provides links to a wide variety of online resources about Tanzania. Topics include adventure travel, African art, languages, Zanzibar sites, and much more.

**British Broadcasting Corporation.** *BBC News.* **2007.**
http://news.bbc.co.uk/ (September 2007).
This website is an extensive international news source. It contains regularly updated political and cultural news. The BBC's country profile of Tanzania is found at http://news.bbc.co.uk/1/hi/world/africa/country_profiles/1072330.stm.

**Central Intelligence Agency. "The World Factbook–Tanzania." 2007.**
http://www.cia.gov/cia/publications/factbook/geos/tz.html (September 2007).
The U.S. Central Intelligence Agency (CIA) provides this general profile of Tanzania. The profile includes brief summaries of the nation's geography, people, government, economy, communications, transportation, and military.

*Insight Guide: Tanzania and Zanzibar.* **London: Insight Guides, 2003.**
This travel guide provides far more than tourist information. Along with lots of color photographs, the authors present helpful and informative text, maps, and guides to the culture and history of the United Republic of Tanzania. They also present a long, special segment about animals and going on safari.

**O'Donnell, Beth.** *Angels in Africa: Profiles of Seven Extraordinary Women.* **New York: Vendome, 2006.**
This book of photo essays presents seven women in sub-Saharan Africa who work to improve conditions in their communities. Tanzania's Edina Yahana is one of them. She has worked since she was thirteen in the field of environmental conservation. She travels teaching villagers how to reduce deforestation by planting trees and by improving fuel efficiency. Text by Kimberley Sevcik accompanies the author's photos.

**"PRB 2007 World Population Data Sheet."** *Population Reference Bureau* **(PRB). 2007.** http://www.prb.org (September 2007).
This annual statistics sheet provides a wealth of population, demographic, and health statistics for Tanzania and almost all countries in the world.

*The Statesman's Yearbook: The Politics, Cultures, and Economics of the World,* **2007. New York: St. Martin's Press, 2006.**
This annual publication provides concise information on Tanzania's history, climate, government, economy, and culture, including relevant statistics.

**Tanzania Tourist Board. 2007.**
http://tanzaniatouristboard.com/ (September 2007).
The Tanzania Tourist Board's official website has almost everything you need to know about visiting this beautiful country. It presents information on Tanzania's wide choice of game reserves and national parks as well as its cities and the many cultures found in the country. Links lead to specific locations, travel advice, and historical and cultural background on this diverse country.

**U.S. Department of State, Bureau of African Affairs. "Background Note: Tanzania."** *U.S. Department of State.* **2007.**
http://www.state.gov/r/pa/ei/bgn/2843.htm (September 2007).
The U.S. Department of State produces this website. It provides a general profile of Tanzania. The profile includes brief summaries of the nation's geography, people, government and politics, and economy.

**Watkins, Thayer. "The Tanganyikan Groundnuts Scheme." N.d.**
http://www.sjsu.edu/faculty/watkins/groundnt.htm (September 2007).
A professor in San José State University Economics Department, Thayer based this in-depth article on Alan Wood's book *The Groundnut Affair* (London: Bodley Head, 1950). It records the famous and economically disastrous efforts by the British government to create groundnut (peanut) plantations in Tanganyika (mainland Tanzania) during the late 1940s.

**Bond, George. The Heritage Library of African Peoples series. New York: Rosen, (1994–1998).**
This series of books presents to younger readers the land, societies, and history of many of Africa's ethnic groups. Three books that cover some of Tanzania's peoples are *Maasai* (1994), by Tiyambe Zeleza; *Makonde* (1998), by John Stoner; and *Sukuma* (1997), by Aimée Bessire and Mark Bessire.

***Bongo Flava: Swahili Rap from Tanzania.* CD. Ray C. Rehema Chamila Video and CD, 2006.**
Juma Nature, Lady J. D., and many other musicians sing about themes ranging from love to politics and just about anything else relevant to life in Tanzania. Lyrics are in Swahili, but the sounds and rhythms of the fourteen songs on this CD will delight even non-Swahili speakers.

**Buettner, Dan. *Africatrek: A Journey by Bicycle through Africa.* Minneapolis: Lerner Publications Company, 1997.**
Buettner and four other team members rode their bikes 11,855 miles across Africa in 1993. Buettner stopped to climb Mount Kilamanjaro in Tanzania, which he describes as a "nightmare" of freezing temperatures and altitude sickness. The author's photographs accompany this interesting adventure tale.

**Lonely Planet Destination Guide. *Tanzania Travel Information.***
www.lonelyplanet.com/worldguide/ destinations/africa/tanzania
This website provides full facts and advice for traveling in Tanzania. It also presents background material on the culture and history of this popular African destination.

**Gurnah, Abdulrazak. *Paradise.* London: Bloomsbury, 1994.**
This novel follows Yusuf, a boy in colonial Tanganyika, growing up enslaved to a powerful Arab trader. The boy is drawn to the merchant's forbidden pleasures, including a garden, which he describes as a kind of paradise. Eventually he must choose between freedom and security.

**MacDonald, Joan Vos. *Tanzania.* Broomall, PA: Mason Crest, 2005.**
This book for younger readers is part of the Africa: Facts and Figures series. It offers an overview of the land, people, and history of Tanzania. Photos, recipes, and project and report ideas accompany the text.

**McQuail, Lisa. *The Masai of Africa.* Minneapolis: Lerner Publications Company, 2002.**
Part of the First Peoples series, this colorful book presents the Masai people. The cattle-herding society follows a traditional lifestyle on the grassy plains of East Africa but has also adopted modern ways, such as creating crafts for the tourist trade.

**Montgomery, Bertha Vining, and Constance R. Nabwire. *Cooking the East African Way.* Minneapolis: Lerner Publications Company, 2002.**
This illustrated cookbook presents recipes from Tanzania and other East African nations. It also supplies information on holidays and festivals, healthy and lowfat cooking tips, and a look at the lands and people of the region.

Further Reading and Websites

**National Website of the United Republic of Tanzania**
http://www.tanzania.go.tz/
This official government site provides information on Tanzania's government, including current news, economic data, census results, and more.

**Reader, John. *Africa*. Washington, DC: National Geographic, 2001.**
This large, photo-illustrated volume is a companion to the eight-hour PBS television series *Africa*.

**Sherrow, Victoria. *Ancient Africa: Archaeology Unlocks the Secret's of Africa's Past*. Washington, DC: National Geographic, 2007.**
Presented with the same full-color photography that illuminates *National Geographic* magazine, this book presents African history through archaeological digs, including those at Olduvai Gorge in Tanzania.

**Smith, William E. *We Must Run While They Walk: A Portrait of Africa's Julius Nyerere*. New York: Random House, 1981.**
This biography of Tanzania's first president is a good place to find out more about the statesman's life and ideas.

**Tanzania Forest Conservation Group**
http://www.tfcg.org
The Tanzania Forest Conservation Group exists to promote the wide biodiversity of the nations forests. Its website presents the group's various projects and programs, including the Amani Butterfly Project, whereby communities raise butterflies for export to live in European and American butterfly houses.

**Twist, Clint. *Stanley and Livingstone: Expeditions through Africa*. Austin, TX: Raintree Steck-Vaughn, 1995.**
British missionary David Livingstone's explorations in Tanzania in the nineteenth century helped to open the land for Europeans. This book for younger readers looks closely at the discoveries and achievements of Livingstone and his fellow explorer of Africa Henry Stanley, the man who "found" Livingstone.

**vgsbooks.com**
http://www.vgsbooks.com
Visit vgsbooks.com, the homepage of the Visual Geography Series®, which is updated regularly. You can get linked to all sorts of useful online information, including geographical, historical demographic, cultural, and economic websites. The vgsbooks.com site is a great resource for late-breaking news and statistics.

**Walker, Sally. *Fossil Fish Found Alive: Discovering the Coelacanth*. Minneapolis: Carolrhoda Books, 2002.**
This is the story of the coelacanth, a fish that survived the wave of extinction that killed the dinosaurs. The scientific drama traces the history of a fish that predates dinosaurs and was thought to be extinct, until one was caught off the coast of South Africa in 1938.

**Wilson, Thomas H. *City-States of the Swahili Coast*. New York: Franklin Watts, 1998.**
Part of the African Civilizations series for younger readers, this book discusses the history and culture of Swahili peoples. The culture stretches along the east coast of Africa, including Tanzania.

**Captions for photos appearing on cover and chapter openers:**

Cover: Wildebeasts continue their annual migration across Tanzania as the sun sets.

pp. 4–5 Giraffes are plentiful in Tanzania's national parks.

pp. 8–9 Stone Town on Zanzibar Island overlooks the Indian Ocean.

pp. 20–21 Ancient human remains have been found in Olduvai Gorge.

pp. 38–39 These Tanzanian children attend primary school in the east central part of the country.

pp. 46–47 A fish market in Tanzania's center of government, Dar es Salaam, bustles with activity.

pp. 56–57 Cloves have been an important cash crop for Tanzania's economy for centuries.

**Photo Acknowledgments**

The images in this book are used with the permission of: © John R. Kruel/Independent Picture Service, pp. 4–5, 15, 50 (left); © XNR Productions, pp. 6, 10; © Tim Graham Photo Library/Getty Images, pp. 8–9; © Brian Seed/Art Directors, p. 11; © Ariadne Van Zandbergen, pp. 13, 20–21, 46-47, 49, 50 (right), 56–57, 58; © Saleh Yahya/Scoopt/Getty Images, p. 16; © Friedrich Stark/Peter Arnold, Inc., p. 17; © Willam F. Campbell/Time & Life Pictures/Getty Images, p. 18; Library of Congress, pp. 24 [LC-USZ62-40651], 25 [LC-USZ61-236], 26 [LC-USZ62-96493]; © Hulton Archive/Getty Images, p. 31; AP Photo, p. 33; AP Photo/Brennan Linsley, p. 35; AP Photo/Khalfan Said, p. 36; AP Photo/Ed Betz, p. 37; © Charlotte Thege/Peter Arnold, Inc., pp. 38–39; © Sean Sprague/Peter Arnold, Inc., p. 40; ©Jorgen Schytte/Peter Arnold, Inc., p. 42; © Clare McNamara, p. 45; © Tony Karumba/AFP/Getty Images, p. 48; © Martin Rose/Bongarts/Getty Images, p. 53; © Jon Arnold Images/SuperStock, p. 60; © Picture Contact/Alamy, p. 61; © Ron Giling/Peter Arnold, Inc., p. 62; © Joerg Boethling/Peter Arnold, Inc., p. 63; ©John Reader/Time Life Pictures/Getty Images, p. 64; © Coyote Fotografx/Art Directors, p. 65; Audrius Tomonis—www.banknotes.com, p. 68.

Front cover: © Mark C. Ross/National Geographic/Getty Images.

Back cover: NASA.